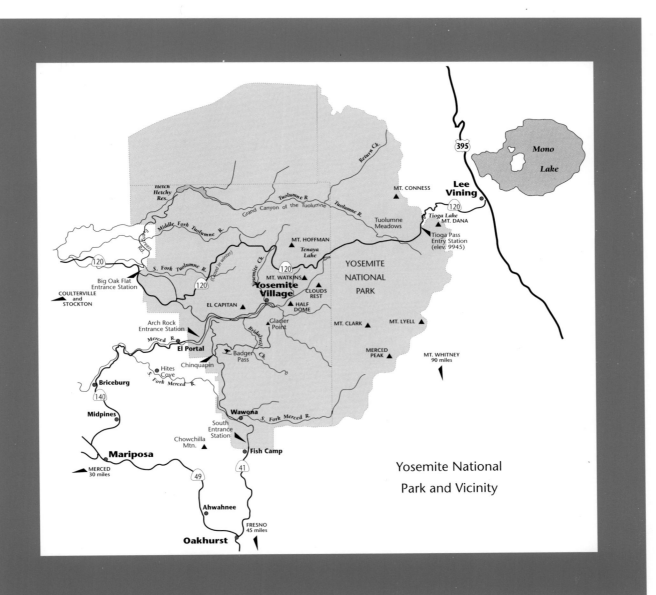

Yosemite National
Park and Vicinity

MAGIC
YOSEMITE
WINTERS

Gene Rose

MAGIC YOSEMITE WINTERS

A CENTURY OF WINTER SPORTS

Gene Rose

Coldstream Press

Cover Photo:
Photograph by John Poimiroo,
Courtesy of Yosemite Concession Services
Back Cover Photos:
Nic Fiore, Courtesy of Yosemite Concession Services
Nordic Skier © Chris Falkenstein
Cover and Book Design: Andrea Hendrick
Contributing Editor: Robert Frohlich
Editors: Laurel Hilde Lippert, Dan Wendin
Printed in Korea by Palace Press

Coldstream Press
P.O. Box 9590
Truckee, California 96162
530-587-4287 Fax: 530-587-9081
E-mail: dwendin@coldstreampress.com
Website: www.coldstreampress.com

Publisher's Cataloging-in-Publication
(Provided by Quality Books, Inc.)

Rose, Gene
    Magic Yosemite winters : a century of winter
sports / Gene Rose. -- 1st ed.
    p. ; cm.
    Includes index
    LCCN: 99-72749
    ISBN: 1-893057-00-3

    1. Winter sports--California--Yosemite National
Park--History. 2. Yosemite National Park (Calif.)
--History.   I. Title.

GV840.7.U6R67 1999   796.9'0979447
            QBI99-1026

TABLE OF CONTENTS

PREFACE

In the fall of 1997 while meeting with the marketing department of Yosemite Concession Services, we learned that Camp Curry would turn one hundred in 1999. We had just released *Mountain Dreamers: Visionaries of Sierra Nevada Skiing*, which included several chapters on Yosemite winter sports and the indomitable Nic Fiore. As that had renewed our fascination with Yosemite, it seemed natural that we publish a book that chronicled the century or more of winter sports in the park.

We are indebted to Keith Walklet and Virginia Chaves, then employees of Yosemite Concession Services, who encouraged us to consider undertaking such a project. At the International Skiing History Association annual meeting in February 1998, we realized that board member Gene Rose may be just the man to prepare the text.

Luckily, Gene was delighted to put to good use his three decades covering the Sierra Nevada, and Yosemite National Park in particular, for the *Fresno Bee*. Perhaps to the dismay of his wife Doris, the project turned into a major effort for the better part of eighteen months. As we neared completion and prepared to send the finished work to the printer, we realized that no other author could have assembled the group of friends and ski buddies who gave life to the stories and provided priceless photographs for use in the book.

We are particularly indebted to Linda Eade and Jim Snyder of the Yosemite Museum and Research Library for their assistance in finding rare old photographs to reprint. Leroy Radanovich had to rise very early on many mornings to avoid road closures into the park to get the negatives needed to prepare our prints. And, finally, Wolfgang Lert, Jim Synder, Dr. Michael Adams, Nic Fiore and Mort Lund took the time to review and comment on the draft text.

Last, but not least, we wish to introduce you to our dear friend and award-winning designer, Andrea Hendrick, who breathed life into the manuscript and photographs to produce a book that is a delight to behold.

Ellie Huggins and Dan Wendin
June 1999

ACKNOWLEDGMENTS

Yosemite's winter sport heritage stands as a towering mountain of action and achievement, with a trail that stretches back more than a century. In seeking that summit, I have been assisted by a special group of individuals who have known and savored the magic of Yosemite winters past. While some of these early pioneers have crossed the final divide, their legacy and love for this snowclad sanctum remains, tucked away in old photo albums and fading newspaper clippings that define their trailblazing ways.

At the top of the pile stands the late Ansel Adams, America's premier outdoor photographer who captured the beauty—and action—not only in eloquent photos but in equally elegant prose. Orland Bartholomew's epic 1928-29 ski trip along the crest of the Sierra has also been preserved. A mountain of assistance came from National Park Service historian James Snyder, whose professionalism and dedication to Yosemite's past stands unrivaled. Research librarian Linda Eade also provided outstanding assistance. Richard Sellars, another park service historian, gave me valuable assistance with the Tresidder papers. The archives staff of the Green Library at Stanford University lent their energies and expertise.

Many others sustained the historical trail. Bill Cahow of Fresno, longtime skier and former head ski instructor, provided an invaluable perspective. And there was Tom Sovulewski, who related his ski trail before crossing the final divide. And years ago, before he left the scene, veteran skier Don Fortune of Fresno gave me copies of the Fresno Ski Club's *Skiesta News*, which provided considerable information on early Yosemite skiing.

I am indebted to Virginia Adams, and her grown children, Anne Adams Helms and Dr. Michael Adams, who provided invaluable guidance and information. Ski champs Boots and Herbert Blatt, who terrorized the ski races in 1930s and 1940s, also shared their heydays on the slopes. Of course there is Nic Fiore, America's most enduring ski instructor who has lived the Yosemite magic for more than fifty years; Jane and Randy Rust, widow and son of the late Leroy "Rusty" Rust, the grand man of Yosemite, shared their historical perspective; David Brower, former publicist and world renowned environmentalist, lent his experiences; Marian and Charles Woessner, other longtime Yosemite residents, offered their recollections; and the Proctor "ski-gals," Mary and her two daughters, Peggy Dean and Nancy Pesmond, filled in other voids.

Marilynn Guske's fabulous postcard collection went a long way in preserving—and recapturing—the visual past. Bernice Shields, cousin of Olympian Brynhild Grasmoen, Wolfgang Lert, Nadine Malm Powers, Charlotte Ewing Wilson and a long line of early racers lent their photos and memories. Joyce Williams Boswell, queen of the 1935 winter carnival, recalled her crowning days; Kirby Gilbert of Seattle found the records of the 1942 national ski races in that distant city; and Yosemite's enduring expert, author and historian Shirley Sargent provided still other gems from the past.

Past and present members of the Yosemite Winter Club also contributed their insights and memories, including Don Reese, Dave Downing, Connie and Ansley Rothell, Ann and Roger Hendrickson, Al Sigal, Jr., Ellie Nishkian, Debbie and Loyd Price, Don and Kay Pitts, Keith Walklet and former park ranger Ron Mackie. Lynn Moss came up with backcountry photos. Several other veterans of the original Fresno Ski Club also assisted, including Larry Huebner, Jack Pieroni, Hal and Eleanor MacMichael Larson, Franklin Knapp and Roger Pirie.

Wayne Merry, Howard Weamer, Helen Harwell, Ed Wade and George Durkee were among the others who lent guidance along the way. George Oliver and his daughter Pat furthered the quest. Art Baggett and Tim Messick, modern mountaineers helped identify their contemporary pathfinders. Not least, of course, is my wife and longtime ski partner Doris, who endured my deviate behavior in pursuing this elusive trail. To countless others who shared their memories and images of this world-class wonder known as Yosemite, I am especially indebted. Thank you,

Gene Rose, April 8, 1999.

INTRODUCTION

Several years ago, while hurrying to Yosemite to cover the rescue of some climbers stranded by snow on the summit of Half Dome, I came into the Valley late in the afternoon, at the conclusion of a major winter storm. The tempest had broken, leaving the Sierra wonderland deep in new snow. The big peaks, the famed landmarks and bowed trees stood resplendent in their winter cloak. As the clouds parted, the majestic alpenglow of artist Albert Bierstadt's grand pallet came streaming in, bathing the enchanting Valley in hues of pinks, purples and blues. It was Yosemite unparalleled—an incomparable Yosemite.

Today, even after fifty years of working and playing within this great national park, that snowy scene remains indelibly etched into the memory bank of this passing observer. I am not alone. Millions of others have their own impressions of this magic winter place.

The late Herb Ewing, one of Yosemite's best known rangers, once shared his reverence for this setting. "Some people look to Yosemite as a religion, a supreme experience, or even a way of life. But they are all wrong. Yosemite is a disease—and it is always fatal."

Yosemite. Few places in the world conjure up so much grandeur, so much beauty. Under a mantle of snow, the great Sierra wonder takes on added depth and diversity. When humans are superimposed upon this snow-covered landscape as winter sports enthusiasts, it reinforces the premise that skiing and ice-skating are the most graceful of all winter sports, especially when set against the splendor of the park.

What brings people to this winter wonderland? Some see it as a world reborn. Others catch a glimpse of a place formed by eons of ice and snow—a page from an unabridged chapter in the evolution of this orbiting jewel known as planet Earth.

I remember a young Finnish girl, an exchange student my family took ice-skating at Yosemite in the 1970s. She was awed by the great chasm with its imposing backdrop of El Capitan and Half Dome. During that visit she confided that none of the ice rinks she had seen in Europe could match the exquisite setting of the Curry rink.

The late Luggi Foeger, one of the great pioneers of Yosemite skiing, once reminisced that the Alps of his native Austria had more spectacular ski slopes than Badger Pass, yet Yosemite's great natural beauty made it a world-class wonder—especially in winter.

While hundreds of books have been written about Yosemite's summer, this is the story of those who embraced the winter season

The Camp Curry ice rink with Half Dome in the background.

and its ultimate delights. Among the hardy explorers of the late 1800s, a small but growing number of adventurers sought the winter magic in skiing, skating and sleighing. In their quest, these aficionados ushered in a whole new world to the fledgling park and, in doing so, created a year-round season for its enjoyment.

Through the years, many of the great names of American skiing touched the snows of Yosemite. For a comparatively brief period, their contributions enabled Badger Pass to stand at the top as the foremost ski area in the nation.

So come, winter is often short. The snows have a way of succumbing to the sun. Grab your skis or skates and join us for a run down memory lane. We'll meet the first, now-departed winter visitors and those early sports pioneers. Along the way we'll encounter others who are still yodeling their love and enthusiasm for this white wonderland. All of them know Yosemite's winter magic.

YOSEMITE—*the ultimate landscape, thundering waterfalls, sheer cliffs and towering trees.*

YOSEMITE—*a magic place—one of the grandest, most sublime settings on earth.*

THE HARDY FEW
1862 - 1917

During winter months, snow settles quickly like a fine dust upon the granite edges surrounding Yosemite's valley floor. Located in a narrow glacial crease near the crest of the Sierra Nevada's western slope, its sculpted mountain architecture bursts upon a visitor with startling suddenness.

John Muir, one of the Valley's earliest advocates, looked at these mountains and remarked, "Every rock seems to glow with life." Snow glistening from the walls of El Capitan, Half Dome, the Three Brothers and Sentinel Rock forms a visual quilt that sparkles and gives life to the winter scenery.

There are only a few paths into Yosemite Valley, and they offer the same spectacular views. However, not until the latter half of the 1800s would venturesome individuals wander into Yosemite's snow-cloaked corridors. Images of the Donner Party's ill-fated winter of 1846 lingered scaringly in the public mind. It was well known that Native Americans of the Sierra Nevada migrated to lower elevations when the shadows grew long in the fall and the first snows fell. Winter loomed to even the most courageous as a season of snow and cold, of hardships and death.

The challenges of winter didn't intimidate James Mason Hutchings. The British-born journalist had led the first summer tourists into Yosemite Valley in 1855. By horseback, they entered the area along a route from today's southern entrance and Wawona. Hutchings first exposed his love for Yosemite in his *Hutchings' Illustrated California Magazine* in 1856. A collection of his articles was published in 1860 entitled *Scenes of Wonder and Curiosity in California*. After marrying in 1860, he hoped to settle in the Valley with his young wife Elvira. In January 1862, he set out from San Francisco to investigate the possibilities of a new life in Yosemite Valley. It was generally believed at the time, Hutchings wrote, that "no one could ever make a permanent winter home in Yosemite, inasmuch as snow from the surrounding mountains drifted into it, as into a deep railroad cut, and filled it half full." But the thoughtful journalist held a keen sense of the

James Hutchings's dream of living amidst the grandeur and majesty of Yosemite finally became a reality when he purchased the Upper Hotel in April 1864. The hotel had first opened in 1859, becoming one of two minimal accommodations in the Valley. Except for a few years in the late 1870s, Hutchings lived in this piece of paradise until 1884.

In 1860, James Lamon stayed on in his small cabin and survived isolation and adversity. He was the first known white man to have spent a winter in the Valley.

power of positive thinking, allowing him to embrace a dream against strong odds.

The determined Hutchings traveled on horseback to seek the true Yosemite of winter. Leaving Stockton, he encountered a severe winter storm. Amid endless rainfall he journeyed seventeen days to reach Coulterville, a mining town only seventy-one miles east of Stockton. At the time little did the intrepid traveler realize he had ridden into the storm of the century, soon to be remembered as the Great Winter of 1861-62. Pressing on, Hutchings discovered bridges and roads washed away. He observed houses, barns and other buildings floating down the Stanislaus River. Finally, he realized the futility of traveling further. He found a boat and made his way back to civilization. His dream remained, however, and, stubbornly, he planned another attempt.

In March, Hutchings teamed with two well-known pioneers familiar with Yosemite, Galen Clark and James Lamon. Clark had settled in Wawona in 1856. Lamon had built the first log cabin in Yosemite

Hutchings's hotel was located on the banks of the Merced River.

Valley in 1859. They left from Clark's ranch, making their first night's camp on ten inches of snow. Progress was exceedingly slow and difficult. Snow deepened as they moved up the mountainside. Without skis or webbed snowshoes, the three travelers plunged through the snow into ankle numbing streams lined by low willows and battled mischievous winds that sent piles of fresh snow cascading from low lying limbs onto their trail. Eventually the formidable obstacles brought their trek to a halt. Hutchings's associates had struggled enough. The two men voted to abandon the effort. Hutchings remained hopeful and argued to continue.

"How can the winter status of the Valley be determined if we wait until spring or summer comes?" Hutchings pleaded to his compatriots. There was no response. The two men had made their decision. After splitting up the food supplies, Hutchings went on alone. For six long days, the solitary hiker pushed his way over the snowy divide towards the enchanted Valley—and to his possible doom. At one point a dejected Hutchings felt he could go no farther and even sat down to write his final farewell to family and friends.

Doggedly, Hutchings moved on. Awakening on the seventh morning of his torturous odyssey, Hutchings climbed to the top of yet another snowy ridge, and, exhausted, peered into the Merced River canyon. "I could look down some three thousand feet upon the river, where to my ineffable joy I could see green grasses growing and flowers blooming—and no more snow. It was a look into paradise," he wrote in his book, *In The Heart of the Sierras*. It would take another three days to work his way up the river to Yosemite Valley.

In 1864, the U.S. government set aside Yosemite Valley and the Mariposa Grove as a reserve for the State of California to "be held for public use, resort and recreation; . . . inalienable for all time." The act marked the first effort toward wilderness preservation. In the fall of that year, Clarence King, a young Yale graduate and geologist with the California Geological Survey, made his way to Yosemite to survey and mark the boundary of the Grant.

The surveyors were under the gun to complete their work before life-threatening snows arrived. One

November morning, while scouting with his assistant Richard Cotter near the base of Mount Clark, they awoke to find their bedding covered by a foot and a half of fresh snow. A heavy snow continued to fall. Hurriedly they packed their animals and struck out for Yosemite Valley.

The storm worsened as they pushed their way through the newly fallen snow. Their animals slipped and skidded, forcing them to be guided by hand. "Suddenly an icy wind swept up the valley, carrying with it a storm of snow and hail. The wind blew with such violence that the whole freight of sleet and ice was carried horizontally with fearful swiftness, cutting the bruised faces of the mules, and giving our own eyelids exquisite torture. . . . Fighting our way against this bitter blast, half-blinded by hard, wind-driven snow crystals, we at last gave up and took refuge in a dense clump of firs which crown the spur by Inspiration Point," wrote King in *Mountaineering in the Sierra Nevada*.

King and Cotter reached camp in the Valley moments before the arrival of a fresh storm front. "The

Ever the adventurous climbers, King and his assistant, Richard Cotter, used their free time to seek out the high vantage points. As the weather gradually changed, they began to push their luck, scrambling to the summits of several peaks.

Clarence King on his climbing rope.

wind shrieked wild and high among the summit crags, it tore through the pine-belts, and now and then a sudden sharp crash resounded through the valley as, one after another, old infirm pines were hurled down before its blast. The very walls seemed to tremble; the air was thick with flying leaves and dead branches; the snow of the summits, hard frozen by a sudden chill, was blown from the walls and filled the air with its keen cutting crystals. At last the very clouds, torn into wild flocks, were swept down into the valley, filling it with opaque hurrying vapors. . . . Sleet and snow and rain fell fast, and the boom of falling trees and crashing avalanches followed one another in an almost uninterrupted roar."

Winter's power descended. The Merced River rose rapidly to flood stage, and fearful that they would be stranded in the mountains, they struggled to Clark's Ranch on the South Fork near Wawona. Yet another storm fell upon them, covering the trail deep in snow. Slogging their way over Chowchilla Mountain, the snow turned to rain. With sighs of relief, the party finally escaped the chilled grip of the storm. "A more drowned and bedraggled set of fellows never walked out upon the wagon road and turned toward Mariposa. Streams of water flowed from every fold of our garments, our soaked hats clung to our cheeks, the baggage was a mass of pulp, and the mules smelled violently of wet hide. Fortunately our note-books, carefully strapped in oil-cloth, so far resisted wetting." Exhausted yet thankful, King and his surveyors had survived.

King's remarkable escape from the elements represented terrors that pioneer families feared most about the Sierra Nevada in winter season. Those whose homes lay in the shadow of mountain peaks all knew of tragedies besetting the few who wandered into the snow covered mountains, never to return. In the succeeding years, even in milder winters, attitudes changed little, and remote regions such as Yosemite piqued little interest as a permanent home.

In the summer of 1855, the first time visitation to the area was recorded, perhaps forty-two tourists traveled to Yosemite Valley. After the creation of the Yosemite Grant, the summer tourist season expanded rapidly.

For awhile Mother Nature relented. The softening weather allowed them to regroup and witness a glorious sunset. But any comfort was short lived as more adverse weather approached. "Setting sunlight smote full upon the stony walls below, and shot over the plateau country, gliding here a showy forest group, and there a wave-crest of whitened ridge. The whole air sparkled with diamond particles; red light streamed in through the open Yosemite gateway, brightening those vast, solemn faces of snow, and intensifying the deep neutral blue of shadowed alcoves."

Yosemite Valley as King and Cotter might have seen it.

© Dewitt Jones

In time, other pioneer settlers joined Hutchings and Lamon as year-round residents of the Valley. The *Mariposa Gazette* reported in February 1874, that "one of the early settlers of Yosemite Valley, Mr. James C. Lamon, left his winter cabin last week and put in an appearance among old friends in Mariposa. Mr. Lamon reports of two to three feet of snow in the valley when he left. The people residing there are in good health and happy and content."

The earliest record of traditional webbed snowshoes at Yosemite reaches back to the winter of 1868. An early winter traveler, probably pioneer Galen Clark, made his way from Clark's ranch at Wawona to Yosemite Valley by way of Summit Meadows and Inspiration Point. Nearing Alder Creek, he ran into unforeseen difficulties. "On my way I struck an unfriendly snag, and finally [ended] up in the top of a small pine protruding through the snow, some distance below. I was not personally very much injured by this perilous feat of backsliding; but upon finding a horrible rent in my pants, with something like a flag of truce hanging half mast in the rear, I felt somewhat embarrassed."

Early in the big winter of 1874-75, one of Yosemite's first trail builders, John Conway, set out from Mariposa to rescue Mrs. John C. Smith, wife of the owner of the Cosmopolitan Saloon in the Valley. She had been badly burned and was in desperate need of medical attention. Conway had also been recently deputized to serve subpoenas in Yosemite Valley for an upcoming murder trial. As if Conway didn't have enough on his mind, a Sierra storm settled directly in his path.

"I set out for Mariposa to receive official papers, thence to Yosemite," Conway recounted years later in the *Mariposa Gazette*. "My outfit consisted of a pair of snow shoes [skis], a pair of rubber boots, and a pair of light calfskin shoes. . . . There was a brisk shower of rain falling, which soon turned to a fearful snow storm. . . . I could scarcely see my way, but continued onward and upward, expecting a lull. I was disappointed. I waded as far a possible, because the fresh-fallen snow would adhere to the snow-shoes if I put them on. . . . It was dark; the snow really smothering; and the wind, blowing a tornado, seemed to go through me like a sieve. My clothing was saturated with perspiration, and I had to keep moving or perish."

The solitary skier traveled through the night, finally taking refuge in a cabin nearly hidden by drifting snow. In the morning Conway remounted his skis and struck out again. The storm raged on unabated but "the temperature had changed—the snow lost its adhesiveness—and the shoes moved along like a charm."

It was three days before an exhausted Conway stumbled into Yosemite Valley. The next morning, much to his relief, the storm had passed.

"I shall ever remember the glory of that morning. The sun rose gradually over the mighty battlements of the east, his rays of light striking the now glittering walls of Yosemite, refracting and flashing from pinnacle to pinnacle, from the South Dome to El Capitan, and from Eagle Peak to Glacier and Inspiration Points, sweeping from Cloud's Rest down to the marvellous gorge, as the orb of day rose higher toward the zenith, flooding its white floor, and chasing away the shadows

Galen Clark and John Conway, whose winter exploits are remembered here.

George Fiske photographed Yosemite in the 1890s. This view of the Three Brothers is what John Conway would have seen as he struggled into the Valley in the winter of 1874-75.

still lurking in the arches of the Cathedral, and revealing the majestic pose of the Three Brothers. It was dazzling— magnificent! . . . Sentinel Rock was robed in a mantle whiter than the whitest lace, and would remind a sentimentalist of a radiant bride, adorned for her husband," John Conway wrote.

Amazingly, Conway made another difficult trip to Mariposa and back before the injured woman could be evacuated from the Valley. With the help of another Yosemite pioneer, innkeeper Fred Leidig, he arranged for horses to take Mrs. Smith from the Cascades on the Merced River via Hite's Cove to Mariposa. It was Conway and five other men, the majority of Yosemite's male population, who moved her by sled down the Valley. Snowfields mixed with thick exposed branches and foliage made their task painstakingly slow. They struggled on to the meeting spot by day's end, where Mrs. Smith's husband waited with horses. Their heroics had saved the pioneer wife.

Photograph by George Fiske

In 1869, the wandering Scotsman John Muir spent the summer in the high country herding sheep. He then stayed on for the winter, building a sawmill in the Valley for Hutchings. The serene winter landscape prompted Muir to take up his pen. In a subsequent article, he described a fierce windstorm "bending and swaying the great pines . . . like a field of wheat, and showering their cones like hailstones. . . . On the north and sunny side it was spring, on the south side there was twelve inches of snow and mid winter—the two seasons separated only by a half a mile of valley."

"Winter has taken Yo-Semite and we are snowbound. The latest leaves are shaken from the oaks and alders, the snowladen pines, with drooping boughs, look like barbed arrows aimed at the sky, and the fern-tangles and meadows are spread with a smooth cloth of snow. . . . Every peak and dome, every niche and tablet had their share of snow. And blessed are the eyes that beheld morning open the glory of the one dead storm. In vain did I search for some special separate mass of beauty on which to rest my gaze. No island appeared throughout the whole gulf of beauty. The glorious crystal sentiment was everywhere. From wall to wall of our beautiful temple, from meadow to sky was one finished unity of beauty, one star of equal ray, one glowing sun, weighted in the celestial balances and found perfect," John Muir wrote in the *New York Weekly Tribune* in March, 1872.

Muir discovered the joy of skiing on the snow-covered slopes of Lake Tahoe. He and friends ventured out on Norwegian snowshoes, the predecessor to today's skis. These wooden longboards or "snow skates" were introduced by Norwegians to the mining camps of the Northern Sierra during the 1850s. One of Muir's companions described the experience as "poetry in action."

The heroics of Norwegian John "Snowshoe" Thompson and his epic trans-Sierra treks on longboards carrying mail between Placerville, California, and Genoa, Nevada, from 1856 to 1876, are legendary. "With these skates, Mr. Thompson, heavily laden, travels over the otherwise almost inaccessible sno clad cliffs and gorges of the Sierras, a distance of from thirty to forty miles a day," reported Hutchings in his *California Magazine* 1857.

Throughout the Sierra, other "snowshoe messengers" also made their appointed rounds on skis, including some of the early Yosemite residents and mail carriers. Throughout the mountain hamlets of those years, skis became a necessity as basic winter transportation. A few adventurous pioneers even found recreation and sport creating some of the world's first ski races. James Hutchings wrote that there was limited use of sleighs pulled by horses that were outfitted with their own "snowshoes."

If old longboards or Norwegian snowshoes could talk, they would reveal tall and heroic tales of mountain messengers and snowbound miners, or of the missions of mercy undertaken by the early pioneers in the Tioga mining area.

No skis throughout the Sierra Nevada were more coveted than those made by Louis DeChambeau, an 1862 native of Quebec, Canada, and an early pioneer in the Mono Lake Basin. By trade he was a millwright and cabinet maker, a well suited background for the task of fashioning skis out of rough timber. His hand crafted skis were such prized items that they commanded the handsome price of $8 a pair.

Longboards at a Yosemite area logging camp.

One day DeChambeau came upon a fellow worker in the Tioga mine at Bennettville who was trying to shape a pair of skis. The man, Norwegian born Erick Erickson, was a talented skier but a poor carpenter. DeChambeau offered his woodworking gifts to help Erickson produce a well crafted pair of skis. A friendship was born. In exchange for DeChambeau's assistance, the Norwegian helped Louis improve his skiing.

The tricky part of shaping the skis was bending the tip, or shovel area. Louis DeChambeau soaked the tip in the hot water reservoir of his wife's wood stove, then used a homemade press to set the bend. He always added his distinctive mark, a hand-carved knob affixed to the tip of each ski. He finished them off by applying varnish or paint, creating a work of skiing art.

Over time, others discovered DeChambeau's craftsmanship and prevailed upon him to manufacture more skis. He used a variety of woods from whatever materials were available. The timber had to be long and straight grained. Often he rustled siding from abandoned houses, fashioning skis in two sizes: nine-foot for the men and seven for the women.

Today, several pairs of vintage DeChambeau skis can be viewed on the walls of the Mono Basin Historical Museum in Lee Vining.

Through the rest of the century, the pattern didn't change. In 1890, the high country surrounding Yosemite Valley was designated a national park, although the Valley and Mariposa Grove remained under the control of the State of California as they were since 1864. They did not become part of the park until 1906. The U.S. Army Cavalry was dispatched to patrol the park for poachers, herders and other possible threats. But the troopers were there only in the extended summer months. With the first sign of snow, they headed back to the Presidio in San Francisco.

Many innkeepers and merchants did likewise, and the one-room elementary school closed for the season, as most of the students went down to the foothills. Most of the estimated 2,000 horses that served the summer trade pulling stages and wagon were taken to the foothills or the San Joaquin Valley for winter pasture. And while horseback riders could handle some snow, any significant accumulation stopped everybody in their tracks.

Occasionally a visiting relative or adventurous traveler would brave the winter elements to see the park or spend the Christmas holiday. But the annual fall migration from Yosemite Valley continued through World War I with few staying on once the snows began to fall.

Compared to today, the early efforts at ice skating and skiing were indeed primitive. The first winter sports fans were true pioneers. Their activities included snowball fights, sledding and skating, and much of their fun began with the construction of their own skis and toboggans.

The late Leroy "Rusty" Rust, Yosemite's first great skier and a lifetime resident who served as postmaster, remembered that his father John Rust worked as a stage driver in the early 1900s, bringing summer visitors to the park from the El Portal rail station. Once autumn arrived, the stage service came to a grinding halt. About the only person coming into the Valley on a regular basis was the mailman. "He had skis stashed at a couple of places along the wagon trail, which he could use as snow conditions warranted—a worker skier."

In the fall of 1908, Charles Wade married Mildred Otelia Amer of Madera. During their honeymoon in Yosemite Valley, he exposed his bride to the wonders of a Yosemite winter and the pleasures and perils of skiing.

"Charles was an avid skier, and during their honeymoon introduced his young bride to cross-country skiing, hoping she would learn to love it as he did," recalled his grandson Ed Wade years later. "That was not to be. Family lore has it that she was upright just long enough to have this picture taken, after which she slipped, fell and announced, 'This is not my cup of tea.' As far as we know that is the only time they wintered over."

In 1893, Nellie Atkinson devised a fine sled for her daughter Dorothy, and using her Norwegian snowshoes, took her daughter for a winter outing.

Today, a few reminders of the legacy of these early residents and visitors can be found in the old family photo albums or the Yosemite museums where old skis and the snowpads used by horses provide lasting reminders of those pioneering days.

The toboggan ride begins...

...and ends.

Celia's father ran Crocker's Station on the Big Oak Flat Road.

Celia Crocker. 1899.

In 1909, a group from Fresno visited the park for some winter fun.

In 1907, the completion of the Yosemite Valley Railroad up the Merced River Canyon was met with great expectation by Valley residents who hoped that it would mark the start of year-round access to the Valley. It was only twelve miles from the end of the railroad at El Portal to the Sentinel Hotel. But during the winter season, the train ran on a reduced schedule and stage service was wet and muddy. The great hope for an all-season Yosemite would have to wait.

We have been here one week they say the snow is nearly all gone along the road now.

"Well, Artie, this is the way some of the roads looked to us on our way in to Yos. on April 7, 1907. We have been here one week. They say the snow is nearly all gone along the road now."

Stephen T. Mather, the first director of the National Park Service, believed strongly,
" Yosemite is a winter as well as summer resort . . ."
It would take the commitment of the Curry Company and its brilliant and capable leader,
Don Tresidder, to implement Mather's vision.

ALL SEASONS YOSEMITE
1917 - 1932

With the establishment of the National Park Service in 1916, winter sports began its momentous evolution in Yosemite Valley. In 1917 workers cleared an 800-foot-long snow slide near the sculptured rock forms rising adjacent to Camp Curry. Youngsters seven to seventy were soon slithering and sliding down its curvy lines with animated giggles. The creative enthusiasts induced the village blacksmith to remove the handles from trash can lids discovered nearby at the Camp Curry dump, or they borrowed large hotel trays to gain speed down the packed run. Its popularity soared. For more than twenty years the slide, aptly nicknamed "Ash Can Alley," proved a constant attraction, evoking the winter outdoor spirit destined to become a Yosemite trademark.

Surrounded by unmatched grandeur while playing in groves of white heather and dwarf willow, no child could have asked to grow up in more playful surroundings. For Tom Sovulewski, born in Yosemite Valley in 1912, this was just the place to propel a child's imagination. His father Gabriel originally traveled into the park as a calvary trooper in 1895 and became the first civilian park supervisor. As a youth during summer months and in between the chores of the tourist season, Tom fished the gravel bars and plunging channels of the Merced River, hiked the granite paths, and explored the meadows and ridges surrounding his majestic home. Sometimes, unfortunately for a young boy, work got in the way of adventuring. By the time he'd grown into adolescence, Tom spent most of his days building trails and campgrounds. Winter was a better time, when the tourists retreated to their homes below, and the park once again was his private playground, heedless to the sirens of an outside world.

"In the mid 1920s there were about eighty or ninety permanent residents in the Valley," Tom Sovulewski recalled before his death in 1996. "There were times where we would be isolated for two or three days; I remember one storm that had us closed down for a week."

Hitching a ride in front of LeConte Lodge in December, 1920.

back then. Some of us had inherited old Norwegian snowshoes or managed to acquire a pair of manufactured skis. Others even used barrel staves with a strip of leather nailed across it. Those were our skis!"

"It was a close-knit community during the winter months. We would often get together for a pot-luck or a party at the old Pavilion; the kids would be put on cots along the sides, and the parents would dance the night through," said Tom. "With the first significant snowfall, the youngsters started getting together to make snowmen, to skate or get involved in a snowball fight. At other times we would go out for ice-skating and snowshoe walks. A few of us had sleds or toboggans. The winters seemed colder then."

Winter months, though sublime and tranquil, and full of discovery and adventure, nonetheless remained harsh and isolated. Tom remembered snow on the Valley floor reaching six feet, making the simplest task a daunting one. Hearty residents learned that snow could be not just a hindrance, but destructive.

For a community that had to endure the hardships of winter, the first stumbling attempts at learning to move on a pair of skis gave release and an opportunity to play amid the snow-covered landscape. Tom recalled schussing down a ski hill shaped from a small moraine near the stables. "The total vertical drop couldn't have been over forty or fifty feet, but that was the Yosemite ski area

Virginia Best, daughter of one of Yosemite's early artists, Harry Cassie Best, and later wife of photographer Ansel Adams, remembers there was skating at Mirror Lake and a spot on the Merced River near the old Sentinel Hotel where the ice was even thicker. She recalls her father, an excellent skater, gliding over the surface of the lake or a small pond near the Yosemite chapel. She also remembers one particular heavy winter in the 1920s when the roof of her father's 1902-built studio collapsed.

It was under the leadership of Stephen T. Mather, the first director of the new National Park Service, that Yosemite's potential as a year-round destination was clearly defined. The Yosemite National Park Company opened Yosemite Lodge in 1915 and the Curry Camping Company had opened its camp in 1899. Mather strongly believed that only a single, financially sound company could create the high quality of overnight facilities necessary to attract the public. In 1925, Mather forced the two companies to merge, much to the consternation of the principals involved. The name of the new company, officially the Yosemite Park & Curry Company, was soon shortened in local conversation to, simply, the "Curry Company."

For Mather, a University of California at Berkeley graduate and devoted Sierra Club member, the only proper course for improving and protecting the emerging national parks was to make them accessible to the public, supported with activities and visitor services. He foresaw public usage as integral to preservation of these special places.

Stephen T. Mather believed Yosemite could become the benchmark for what a national park should be, relying on a partnership between the park service and a year-round committed concessionaire.

"Yosemite is a winter as well as summer resort. . . . That it has not been more patronized during the winter months is due partly to limited accommodations and partly to lack of publicity," he said.

Stephen T. Mather with Jennie Foster Curry. Known to everyone as Mother Curry, she and her husband, David, founded the Curry Camping Company in 1899.

Speaking eloquently at a parks conference several years earlier, Mather said, "Scenery is a hollow enjoyment to a tourist who sets out in the morning after an indigestible breakfast and a fitful sleep on an impossible bed."

It would, however, take the commitment of the Curry Company and its brilliant and capable leader, Don Tresidder, to implement Mather's vision.

A dozen years before the merger, Tresidder, a native of Indiana, had traveled west on vacation with his sister Oliene following his first year of premed studies at the University of Chicago. When a flood delayed their train near Fresno, a fellow passenger recommended that Don and his sister visit nearby Yosemite. Whether it was their inevitable fate or simply the suggestion of a stranger, the two left the train and made their way to the park for what was intended to be a brief look.

Tresidder discovered wonders he never thought imaginable. The long and dramatic cascades of Bridalveil, Vernal, Nevada and Yosemite Falls spread in broad sheets of mist which arched in thundering rainbows. Subalpine belts of whitebark pine, red fir and lodgepole pine stood guard over boundless acres of pristine beauty. His native Indiana had nothing to compare. Such magnificent scenery tugged at Tresidder, enticing him to stay on for the summer.

Luckily, the affable Tresidder met Rufus Lot Green, a Stanford University math professor and dedicated visitor to the park. Green took a liking to the Tresidders and recommended them to David Curry, proprietor of the Curry Camping Company. That summer, Tresidder worked as a porter while Oliene spent her time hostessing.

Well-educated, articulate and capable, Tresidder was encouraged by his newfound friends, especially Professor Green, to stay in the West and continue his medical studies at Stanford University in Palo Alto. When the lack of finances stalled Tresidder's decision, Green invited the soon-to-be architect of Yosemite's future to live with the Green family while he attended the university.

It was a decision Tresidder would never regret. He attended Stanford for the next two years, returning during summer vacations to work in Yosemite. The First World War interrupted life in 1917 and, like many others, Tresidder joined the war effort, becoming a pilot in the newly organized Signal Corps and spending his service time in California and Texas.

After the 1918 armistice, Tresidder returned to civilian life. He resumed his medical schooling at Stanford, but life in Yosemite began to consume as much energy. The park beckoned him each summer. Yosemite offered more to Tresidder than just a captivating setting. During his Yosemite summers, he met and fell in love with Mary Curry, the attractive daughter of his employers, David and Jennie Curry. Mary had graduated from Stanford in 1915 and pursued graduate work at Yale University. The collegians shared a deep love of Yosemite. Together they hiked through the park's verdant subalpine meadows. Their relationship blossomed as they wandered beneath Yosemite's cathedral-like reaches.

Courtesy of Stanford University Archives and Ann Grishaw Mosser

Don and Mary Tresidder were married at Camp Curry in 1920.

Tresidder's responsibilities increased when he married into the Curry family, but he was far from a shallow opportunist. He carried a thoughtful perspective, dignity and seriousness toward his work. With an engaging personality and a caring nature, his innovations and presence would define Yosemite's future, and, indeed, stand the test of time. Although he received his medical degree, he would never practice medicine. Like so many people who upon seeing a mountain want to climb it, Tresidder sought to create a park worthy of Yosemite's powerful beauty. Combining a sharp business acumen with a disarming personality, he was able to make Yosemite's shaky merger of two warring companies a reality. Within the space of a dozen years, Tresidder, the once wayward pilgrim from Indiana, graduated from luggage handler to president of the Yosemite Park & Curry Company.

By the mid 1920s the park service paved the roads in Yosemite Valley. In 1926 the all-weather highway, known today as Highway 140, was completed through the Merced River Canyon from Mariposa. The automobile, maligned as "the blunt-nosed mechanical beetle" by John Muir, and even banned from the park only a decade earlier, now entered the Valley any time of the year. With convenient year-round access, Yosemite began to grow into a community.

Yosemite was quickly gaining additional national and, indeed, worldwide attention. Visitors streamed into the park summer and winter, initially catching Tresidder's limited staff unprepared. During January 1927, park visitation exploded to nearly seven times more than the previous year. On one day alone, February 13, 1927, a record 875 cars chugged into the Valley, while only a handful had managed to gain entrance a year earlier.

THE AHWAHNEE

After famed English aristocrat Lady Astor refused to spend a night in Yosemite because of the park's rudimentary lodging facilities, Stephen T. Mather knew that something grand had to be built. He directed the Curry Company to undertake construction of a hotel whose world-class lodging would allow visitors luxury and comfort amidst the most beautiful scenery in the world. The magnificent Ahwahnee Hotel opened July 14, 1927. Its name taken from the Miwok word, "Ahwahneechee," for the dwellers of the Valley, the Ahwahnee was built at a then staggering cost of one million dollars. Other facilities also needed upgrading. The overriding question was how to pay for it all. Tresidder was up to the challenge. "The construction of the Ahwahnee was where Don first displayed and sharpened his administrative skills that were so valuable later," recalled Stanford colleague Thomas D. Spragens. "He orchestrated every detail of the construction, working with the architects and the designers and the contractors and the budget people, and bringing them all together."

The ice was thick on Mirror Lake this day in 1928.

The Ahwahnee Hotel opened its doors on July 14, 1927.

From its opening day in 1927, the luxurious Ahwahnee Hotel was a place where well-heeled and connected individuals could gather to enjoy the grandeur of Yosemite. A grand hotel for a grand park.

Tresidder recognized the need for inspiring activities to induce overnight guests to visit Yosemite throughout the year. The newly constructed highway into the park, combined with the Ahwahnee's "Great Lounge," solarium, luxurious roooms and 130-foot-long dining hall, boosted winter visitor counts. Still, too few stayed overnight. The winter season proved a "hard sell," even for a place as beautiful as Yosemite. Discouraged, many park administrators were ready to give up. At one point, a board member even suggested shutting down the concessions after the summer season.

The Ahwahnee's Great Lounge.

The Ahwahnee clientele demanded something special. During his Stanford years, Tresidder was exposed to the social and cultural whirl of the Bay Area. His marriage and rise to the head of the company prompted an invitation to join the exclusive Bohemian Club. Tresidder particularly enjoyed its special Christmas event called "Hi Jinx." He concluded that the Ahwahnee needed something similar: a festive holiday pageant to complement the splendor of Yosemite's newest cathedral. Such an attraction would serve as a magnet and as an alternative for those who might not like snow or winter sports. Thus, the idea of the Ahwahnee's Bracebridge dinner was born.

For the initial production on Christmas Day 1927, Tresidder invited singers from the Bohemian Club festival to the Ahwahnee. He hired Garnett Holme, a professional dramatist, to develop a pageant based on Washington Irving's "Bracebridge Hall," set against the splendor of the squire's Tudor manor. This first event was a resounding triumph. Unfortunately for all involved, success was marred by Holme's sudden death a few months later.

Don and Mary Tresidder preside at the 1928 Bracebridge pageant at the Ahwahnee.
Everyone dressed in wigs and formal wear for the festive occasion.
After the death of Garnett Holme the next spring, Tresidder turned to a youthful and
talented Bay Area musician and photographer, Ansel Adams, to orchestrate the event.

For years, even before they were married, Don and Mary Tresidder ventured out on skis, skates or snowshoes. They found mutual enjoyment in exploring the Yosemite winter. He, particularly, enjoyed the thrills and spills that went with skiing. While business served as a primary compulsion in his life, Tresidder was unswervingly devoted to skiing as a new and exciting sport. "No one was more exuberant than he, gliding through the forest, yelling and whooping for sheer ecstasy, twisting between trees, dodging branches, leaping logs. Nor was anyone more sensitive to surrounding beauty than his wife, especially while ski touring," observed Yosemite historian Shirley Sargent.

In 1928, the Curry Company sent the Tresidders to the Second Winter Olympic Games in St. Moritz, Switzerland. There, surrounded by the world famous peaks of the Alps, the Tresidders observed joyous throngs of spectators rallying the competitors with cheers and a symphony of clanging cowbells. The festivities and enthusiasm were contagious fun. The couple returned home, charged up with a new and

Don and Mary Tresidder stroll on one of the trails in the Valley.

enlarged vision of what Yosemite might be. They dreamed Yosemite could become the "Switzerland of the West." Snowplay and winter recreation would act as the magnet to draw visitors to the park.

The International Olympic Committee designated the United States as host of the 1932 Winter Olympic Games. Knowing that a site in this country was still to be determined, the Tresidders

returned from Europe with the 1932 Games on their minds and with Yosemite as the place.

In the fall of 1928, Tresidder formed the Yosemite Winter Club to "encourage and develop all forms of winter sports [and] to advertise and exploit the great advantages, beauties and healthy benefits of winter in the California Sierra to all lovers of outdoor life." In its seventy-year span to the present day, the club has played a leading role in the evolution of winter sports in California.

Sponsored by the Curry Company, the Winter Club became a popular social organization stocked with many of Tresidder's well-connected friends from San Francisco and Los Angeles. It also included several members from the upper echelons of the National Park Service. Tresidder was the first president; Horace Albright, acting superintendent of Yosemite, was the honorary president. Other club members included Yosemite residents and prominent Californians of the period's upper social circles.

"Get them in and make them happy."
Don Tresidder

Support for winter sports and tourism also came from the influential and powerful Southern Pacific Railroad which recognized the potential for boosting passenger travel during the slow winter months. The Yosemite Valley Railroad ran from Merced on S.P.'s line in California's Central Valley to El Portal. The connection was ready-made for winter recreation.

As a Yosemite Valley teenager, John Degen had the job of sending the toboggan riders down the new slide. "It was a pretty advanced slide," Degen remembers. "At the top, there was a movable platform that could be tripped so that the back edge would rise, sending the tobogganers down. We used three or four lanes and we alternated from one to another so the tobogganers wouldn't run into each other. Once they reached the bottom, riders would move the toboggan onto a return conveyor. It had a cog on a power-driven chain that would catch the back edge of the toboggan and haul it back to the top."

A new toboggan slide was built on a site just west of Camp Curry. The modern four-track facility served a new generation of winter sports enthusiasts.

The south side of the Yosemite Valley, under the shadows of Glacier Point, was a naturally colder area. There, the Camp Curry parking lot was lined with sandbags and flooded, creating a huge ice-skating rink. Stoneman Meadow, just across the road from Camp Curry, and the road past the stables to Mirror Lake, developed into hubs of traditional winter activities such as dogsled rides, sleighing and skijoring (skiing behind a horse with a tow rope). Hockey games, curling, and speed and figure skating also proved to be very popular. A small ski jump was built on the moraine near the stables which reportedly allowed a jumper to soar sixty feet. Snowshoe races were held at Stoneman Meadow, and even chief ranger Forest Townsley and his wife joined in the fun.

Skijoring under the watchful eye of Half Dome.

The Tresidders invested most of their time toward turning Yosemite into a world-class sports center. From the outset, as with many other winter sports pioneers, they envisioned skiing as only ski touring and jumping. They observed the influential San Francisco-based Sierra Club organizing popular winter forays to the Lake Tahoe and Truckee areas of California that featured winter walks on snowshoes and skis. Downhill skiing, on the other hand, had yet to awaken much of a following. From their narrow vantage point, the Tresidders thought the future of Yosemite's winter allure was in ski touring.

With the hope of an Olympic bid, Tresidder hired Ernst des Baillets, a Swiss national he had met during his European trip, as the park's winter sports director. Together they devised an ambitious program of winter activities, including skating and tobogganing. They had a simple goal: Yosemite as the host of the Winter Olympic Games.

Ernst des Baillets had proved his expertise in promoting winter sports at the Snowbird Club in Lake Placid, New York, and the Chateau Frontenac in Quebec City, Canada. He is shown here presenting trophies to Gladys Brittain and Thomas Meagher, California Speed Skating Champions in 1931.

Mary Tresidder recalled Jules Fritsch as a "stocky little Swiss, utterly devoted to snow and mountains, with a profound knowledge of Alpine snow conditions. He was a dedicated ski teacher who counted that day lost when he couldn't assemble his group of pupils to practice a few stems, telemarks or christies."

Entering the winter of 1928-29, Tresidder established the Yosemite Ski School. The school, the first in the West, was directed by Jules Fritsch, a transplanted Swiss skier and dedicated mountaineer. The park could not have made a better choice. He had more than fifteen years of experience at the Swiss ski centers in Engadine, Davos and Berner Oberland.

Fritsch's staff included fellow countryman, Ralph de Pfyffer, German Wolfgang Greeven, and Gordon Hooley, a well-known Canadian skier and jumper who had established his reputation at Revelstoke in British Columbia. Greeven and Hooley gave ski jumping exhibitions almost every weekend. Hooley doubled as an ice-skating instructor, and each talented athlete also guided ski tours.

Even with the introduction of new activities in the Valley, Ash Can Alley continued to be the most popular. For many first-time visitors the fun ride was their introduction to winter sports. "Ash Can Alley still remains the most fun and has contributed more to the pleasure of our winter visitors than all other sports combined," the National Park Service newsletter reported in January 1929. "It requires the work of from four to seven rangers to handle traffic on the roads near the slide and to instruct people how to ride, besides keeping the tracks in good working order." Nearby at the skating pond on the Merced River, with the ice ten to fifteen inches thick, there was an average of eighty-five skaters on a typical weekend.

In the spring of 1929, a wave of excitement spread over the country as people began speculating about which site would be selected to stage the coveted 1932 Winter Olympic Games. Competition to host the first Winter Games in the United States grew into an intense contest. Three established winter snowplay areas, Yosemite and

Cars at the bottom of Ash Can Alley.

"Ranger Freeland, who was recently put in charge of the Ash Can Alley, reports a total number of 1,634 signatures on his register for the week, and a total of 1,352 over the weekend of Friday, Saturday and Sunday," the National Park Service newsletter reported.

Lake Tahoe in California, and Lake Placid near Whiteface Mountain in New York, emerged as the prime contenders. Yosemite pointed to its lodging. Lake Placid countered with the promise of newly constructed modern facilities. The Lake Tahoe promoters boasted of a three-million-dollar bankroll that could build anything the International Olympic Committee (I.O.C.) wanted. Using the expertise of Lars Haugen, a seven-time Class A National Jumping Champion, hopeful Tahoe organizers had already built a sixty-five-meter ski jump at "Olympic Hill" at what is now Granlibakken Resort in Tahoe City.

At Yosemite, Don Tresidder ordered the construction of a new 60,000-square-foot ice rink to support both figure and speed skating events. The structure allowed for eight laps per mile. While Yosemite could brag about its overnight accommodations, there were few other venues to support most of the Olympic events. Skiing, Tresidder figured, required little more than a cross-country course and a ski jump. He was noticeably silent about

a bobsled run. Tresidder predicted that ice-skating would win Yosemite's bid for the Winter Games.

As one of California's prime tourist attractions, Yosemite had the political muscle that Lake Tahoe lacked, with support that ran all the way from the White House to the director of the National Park Service. When the decision was made in January 1929, Yosemite was the California contender.

In March, the California delegation journeyed to the I.O.C.'s final meeting at Lausanne, Switzerland. However, the state's past failure to embrace snow and winter sports proved fatal. Although the Yosemite delegation produced a motion picture of beautiful snow-covered mountains, its presentation failed, coming across to voters as more imagery than substance. Instead, the I.O.C. was impressed by Lake Placid's proven track record. Strongly supported by New York state and its nearby communities, the resort had staged winter carnivals and other events for a decade. I.O.C. dignitaries felt California had little experience in conducting competitive events, in conducting competitive events,

particularly in winter sports. Lake Placid won the committee's vote, becoming the first American site to host the Winter Olympics.

Although disappointed, Ernst des Baillets, Yosemite's director of winter sports, couldn't blame the I.O.C. for their decision. "It was the complete lack of duly affiliated associations governing each phase of winters sports—skiing, skating, hockey and so on," he later admitted, "and the consequent lack of experience in holding organized competitions in these sports that wisely led the International Olympic Committee to reject California's invitation and award the next Olympic Winter Games to Lake Placid."

California snow enthusiasts woke up with the I.O.C.'s rejection of their Olympic dreams. Almost overnight, the California State Chamber of Commerce reversed its previous course and began to embrace winter sports as a viable, economic and popular commodity. It hired Jerry Carpenter, an enthusiastic skier from San Francisco, to be editor of the chamber's magazine and principal promoter in developing winter sports programs. Not

surprisingly, Carpenter, whose good work soon earned him the title of "Father of Skisport" in the Golden State, signaled the chamber's new direction by publishing a banner across the December 1929 issue proclaiming "California's Newest Industry—Winter Sports." Carpenter wrote inside the slick-paper magazine, "California offers her residents and tourists a complete program of winter sports that promises to equal, and in some respects exceed, the winter sports of the most famed European, Canadian and Eastern Resorts."

The Yosemite winter schedule expanded to include the California Amateur Speed Skating Championships. Delayed for a week because of heavy snow, the races were held on February 2, 1930. Two weeks later, Yosemite hosted the Pacific Coast Intercollegiate Winter Games. Three of California's largest schools, the University of California at Berkeley, the University of Southern California and the University of California at Los Angeles competed in the three-day contest. Tresidder prevailed upon President Herbert

Hoover, a Stanford University alumnus and a longtime admirer of Yosemite, to lend his name to the winter activities by sponsoring the Hoover Cup, awarded to the winner of the games. Hoover's association immediately gave credibility to Yosemite's quickly emerging programs.

With the addition of the new rink, Yosemite became the premier ice-skating center in California. Although skating rinks could be found at a half-dozen California cities, few could match the natural setting of Camp Curry. Of the nearly 125-member California Skating Association in 1930, nearly a fourth hailed from Yosemite. In March, Yosemite skaters dominated at the state's first indoor skating competition in San Francisco. Familiar Yosemite competitors Leroy "Rusty" Rust, Gabe Sovulewski Goldsworthy and Gordon Hooley captured medals.

In the fall of 1930, Tresidder and Ernst des Baillets helped convince the California Chamber of Commerce to summon representatives from mountain communities to organize the

Skiers on the Camp Curry ski hill with the jump in the background.

California Ski Association. The October meeting was held at the Palace Hotel in San Francisco's financial district. The sixteen-member group, which included such notables as Scotty Allen, world famous sled dog racer from Soda Springs, Burt A. Cassidy, newspaper publisher and state senator from Auburn, influential journalist William B. Berry, Wilbur Maynard of Truckee, Oscar Jones of Soda Springs, and Dr. W.F. Durfer of Auburn, unanimously elected the Auburn Ski Club's Wendell Robie president. Vice-presidents chosen included Tresidder and J. B. Hanson of the Viking Ski Club of Los Angeles.

Robie's first act was to ask for recognition and admittance of the newly born alliance into the National Ski Association.

For Tresidder it was a crowning moment. No longer was his a voice in the winter wilderness. From north to south, newspapers sang the praises of snow and winter sports. Such promising attitudes prompted Tresidder to predict that, "Within a very few years there will be found in the Sierra Nevada of California the outstanding winter resorts of America."

A speed skating race in progress.

The influential San Joaquin Tourist and Travel Association soon joined the cheerleaders. On January 10, 1931, more than 3,700 people entered the park for the San Joaquin Valley-Sierra Winter Sports Carnival, undoubtedly the largest winter turnout Yosemite had seen. There were skating competitions, snowshoe races at Camp Curry meadows and curling matches. The famed firefall illuminated the face of Glacier Point as a prelude to the highlight of the evening, the crowning of Lois Laveen as Sierra Winter Sports Queen. Part of the festivities included eighty-five skaters in beautiful and unique costumes parading around the ice rink in the grand march.

The following weekend Yosemite hosted the second annual California Outdoor Amateur Speed Skating Championships. At month's end, the West Coast speed skating tryouts for the 1932 Winter Olympic Games were hosted at the Camp Curry rink. Ironically, given the emphasis that had been placed on ice-skating in Yosemite's Olympic bid, no local skater finished within the times required for the final tryouts in the East.

Marion Starr and Leroy "Rusty" Rust, juvenile champions of the California Outdoor Amateur Speed Skating Championship in January 1931.

Through the mid 1930s, Yosemite's ice-skating program continued its climb into national prominence. The new and enlarged skating rink, along with professional skating instruction, produced top results. Yosemite youngsters were making great strides, no longer fumbling and flailing on the ice. Valley school children remember practicing long hours under the watchful and demanding eye of Winter Club skating coaches, eventually learning through torturous practice the dreaded compulsory figures. Jane Rust, widow of Leroy "Rusty" Rust, recalls that, as a youngster, the "boy wonder" of Yosemite participated in skating, skiing and ice hockey coached by Ernst des Baillets and Ralph de Pfyffer. Year after year, whether on ice or snow, Rusty was the one to beat in Yosemite winter competition.

Even with its outstanding programs, not everyone involved became a world-class skater. As a school boy in Yosemite Valley during the 1930s, John Degen remembers skating at the early winter carnivals. "They came over to the school, put costumes on us and took us over to the ice rink," he recalled. "We put on skates at the rental shop and were led out on the ice to do a skit we had done as part of a school play. I had never been on skates before and all I can remember is falling down."

The Curry Company and Winter Club continued staging a special event every winter weekend. Ice hockey flourished throughout the 1930s aided by a steady stream of professional teams and collegiate and local exhibitions. Yosemite hosted several prestigious skating championships. Nevertheless, by the end of the decade, Camp Curry's dominant programs and high level skating competitions began to lose their prominence. New indoor rinks were appearing at more California locations, and outdoor rinks found it more difficult competing with the consistent and superior artificial ice. Although sanctioned skating events were held for several more years at Yosemite, it became apparent that the park's day of big ice skating extravaganzas had passed.

Despite these successes and popularity, Tresidder still faced huge obstacles to making Yosemite a year-round destination. His work

was made more difficult by the Great Depression. To Tresidder, no matter what the obstacle, problems were to be solved, not avoided. He organized a marketing team to actively promote the park. Ansel Adams's photographs depicting Yosemite's breathtaking winter settings and marvelous events were bound into large photo albums and then sent to key media across the country.

The sales tools were a valiant attempt, but the inconsistency of winter, whether too much snow or not enough, affected visitor attendance. Midweek winter bed counts were often low. Even the grand Ahwahnee Hotel could not make Yosemite a destination resort. The company lost money in both 1931 and 1932. Once again, critics considered shutting down concessions and not reopening until Easter.

Just as the opening of the all-weather highway from Merced helped make Yosemite Valley into an all-season park, a new road from Fresno would launch Yosemite into the bright future of downhill skiing. Badger Pass was about to burst onto the winter scene.

Courtesy of Ann Grishaw Mosser

A skier works his way up the slope of Mount Watkins. This was the Tresidders' 1931 Christmas card.

Tobogganing in the Valley.

Dog sleds were common and a lot of fun in those years.

Resting after snowshoe trip to Glacier Point.

Marilynn Guske of Fresno
has been collecting
postcards for decades.
These are just
a few from her collection
showing people
at play in Yosemite in the
1920s and early 1930s.

YOSEMITE POSTCARDS

Ice-skating on the Merced River in back of the old Sentinel Hotel.

At the bottom of the toboggan slide.

The Chinquapin run is a true test for stemming, for the trail is too narrow to permit Christianias.
In late afternoon, when the run becomes a bit iced, even professionals can thrill to the speed of its course.
Its great popularity certainly had something to do with the ski hut at the end of the run
where skiers gathered to meet friends over a hot drink and food.

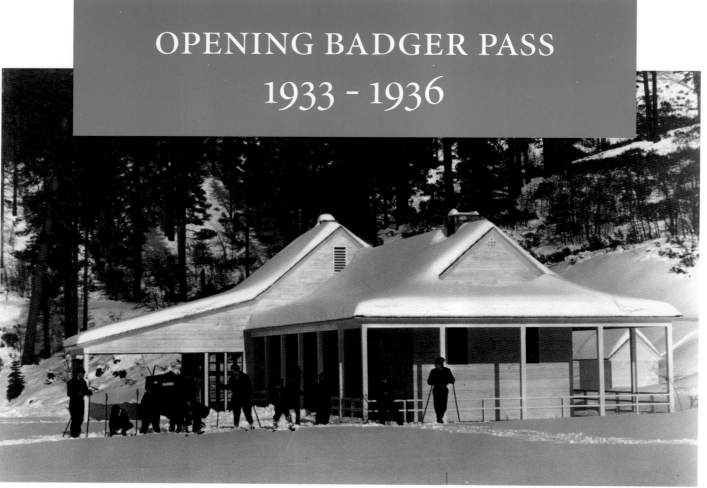

OPENING BADGER PASS
1933 - 1936

The Ski Hut at Chinquapin opened in 1933.

By the early 1930s, the Ski Hill's enchanting slope in Yosemite Valley was being tested by the increasing scope of burgeoning Winter Club events. In lean years, its relatively low 4,000-foot elevation didn't provide consistent snow conditions. The gentle area no longer challenged many visitors. As one club member remarked, "It was too low, too horizontal or too vertical."

Adventurous skiers began probing north-facing snowfields in the higher elevations above the Valley's south rim. There, ridges revealed slopes rich in snow. Don Tresidder saw the area's promise for developing skiing. He knew of the cable tramways in the Alps. He hired lift consultants to explore the possibility of something similar from Yosemite Valley to both Glacier Point and north to the Snow Creek Chalet and beyond to Tenaya Lake. The idea of ascending from Happy Isles in the Valley to Glacier Point was given serious consideration. Tresidder submitted a plan, arguing that a tramway journeying up the short but steep path would be inconspicuous, compared to projected roads, and less destructive to the scenery. The economics of the Depression made any such scheme fiscally difficult at best and, in any event, the park's advisory board rejected the idea.

Nevertheless, Glacier Point's expansive views and marvelous country offered a landscape unlike anything in the world. "If Glacier Point with its beautiful hotel were available in the wintertime, Sentinel Dome with its heavy snowfall could be made to rival St. Moritz," National Park Service director Stephen T. Mather once observed. He insisted, however, that nothing should blemish the breathtaking scenery of Yosemite's canyon walls.

"The Valley didn't always have snow in the winter, but Chinquapin had both snow and a slope. It was a big step forward," recalled Tom Sovulewski.

Even though not yet officially opened, the Wawona Tunnel was usable beginning in the fall of 1932. At Chinquapin, an area twelve miles south of the Valley, company crews cleared brush and trees at the 6,000-foot site before autumn snows fell, delighting anxious skiers. "The Valley didn't always have snow in the winter, but Chinquapin had both snow and a slope. It was a big step forward," recalled Tom Sovulewski.

The first historic race at Chinquapin challenged Winter Club members on January 26, 1933. Fourteen eager skiers went against each other and the clock for the first time. Barney Moen won the slalom and Bill Stark captured the downhill. Gabe Goldsworthy and Emily Hoag competed on an equal footing with the men in the slalom. Don Tresidder fell in the downhill but finished a respectable seventh in the slalom.

Club members continued to explore the surrounding terrain. Six miles up Glacier Point Road, west of Badger Pass above Monroe Meadows, Sovulewski and his fellow enthusiasts discovered rolling, north-facing terrain lined

Ski instructors for the 1933-34 season: Ralph de Pfyffer, Earl Myr, Jimmy Connell, Gordon Hooley and, the boss, Jules Fritsch.

Struggling to keep balance for the hand-cranked camera on the run at Chinquapin.

Photograph by Pop Lavel

with stands of tall conifers leading to a protected meadow below. At 7,300 feet elevation, the 360-degree view from the top revealed a jagged horizon of snowy ranges. The possibilities were obvious to everyone, Sovulewski recalled. "Tresidder went up and had a look. He apparently liked what he saw. Soon the Curry Company was running its eighteen-passenger White touring cars up there. That was the beginning of Badger Pass."

After the Wawona Tunnel opened in June 1933, the untapped alpine slopes were accessible to all. The lack of amenities didn't detract from the adventure. Club members embraced the new area with unchecked enthusiasm. Tom Sovulewski, who went on to be one of Yosemite's best skiers during the 1930s, recalled, "By having to climb the hill, we didn't get many runs in those days. But we did have fun. We would tramp up the hillside, skis over our shoulders. At the top, we would put our skis on, then head downhill, fall, get up, go a short way and fall again—then getting up and doing the same thing over and over again. Skiing was an exercise in repeated falls."

The annual tussle for the Hoover Cup in the Pacific Coast Intercollegiate Winter Games began in 1930 with only ice-skating and hockey. In later years it would be truly "Pacific Coast," but at first it was only teams from the University of Southern California and the University of California at Los Angeles and at Berkeley, with Loyola University soon joining in. An early winter insured good ice and snow for the fifth running of the games in December 1933.

A cross-country race had been added the year before and this year's race ushered in the season at Badger Pass. It was won for the second straight year by Cal's Alex Hildebrand, oldest son of the skiing Hildebrand family.

Winter Club events mushroomed at the larger new area. In early January, thirty entrants competed in the Winter Club slalom and downhill. Primitive by today's standards, the course was marked by starting pole and little else. Racers charged down the run in a curious manner, some with arms windmilling through the air in reckless abandon. Injuries, disqualifications and broken

To many, skiing's new freedom was beyond simple description. Fresno native and future ski instructor Bill Cahow began skiing on handmade skis as a teenager during the winter of 1933-34. At that time, enthusiasts sped downhill at "Old Badger," just east of today's lodge. Bill remembers a snow-covered mountain and a couple of outhouses stuck in the trees. And there were lots of trees which skiers maneuvered around on short, gentle runs. These pioneers understood that they were setting the course toward something new. Yosemite had seen the future, and it was Badger Pass and downhill skiing.

equipment were not uncommon. Finish times varied widely between competitors, but some of the more accomplished skiers posted exceptional results.

Alex Hildebrand and Ed Janss were the stars of the meet. The Winter Club newsletter reported, "Both boys displayed wonderful form in their skiing. During the races, snow fell almost continually which frequently handicapped the skiers in making turns. . . . Louise Hildebrand was by far the best of the women skiers, and her time compared very favorably with the men's."

The most famous skier to dash down the hill on that wintry day was Charlie Chaplin. The famed celebrity impressed the avid spectators with his unsuspected athletic ability in the downhill race, although he finished well behind the leaders. "The crowd watching the meet was fortunate in having an opportunity to see Charlie Chaplin, the moving picture actor, perform on skis. Mr. Chaplin is an enthusiastic skier and entered all the ski events, proving many thrills for the spectators," one observer noted.

Built in 1933, the lunchroom at the Chinquapin service station doubled as a day lodge for skiers. Ski runs were cut from Badger Pass to the lodge and down Strawberry Creek to Wawona Road. These were immediate hits even with the need for a car shuttle. An experimental electric lift was installed at Badger for the 1934-35 season. Carrying only a few skiers at a time, the cable-drawn toboggan was a big success— a welcome alternative to laborious sidestepping.

During the early 1930s, the National Park Service strongly supported Tresidder's wide-ranging winter sports programs. Stanford alumni President Herbert Hoover and Interior Secretary Ray Lyman Wilbur, soon to be president of the university, believed strongly in winter recreation for Yosemite.

However, the government's attitude changed drastically in 1933 when Franklin Roosevelt took office. He appointed Harold Ickes to replace Wilbur. Ickes, a central figure in Roosevelt's "New Deal," was an able and responsible administrator. Yet, he was also

Facilities or not, ten thousand skiers visited Badger Pass in the 1934-35 season.

an ardent preservationist who said, "If I had my way about national parks, I would create one without a road in it, . . . a place where man would not try to improve upon God." During the long Roosevelt administration, Yosemite never regained the political clout it had enjoyed under Hoover's regime.

Business was booming, but the lack of adequate facilities was becoming an overwhelming problem. Badger could only offer snacks to its guests and the outhouses were rudimentary at best. Although the political climate in Washington wasn't helpful, Tresidder continued to seek approval for construction of a ski lodge complete with restrooms, dining, ski rental, ski school and other services. Estimated to cost $32,000, the lodge had a powerful ally in Yosemite superintendent Charles G. Thomson. Through Thomson's lobbying efforts with Ickes, funding was approved for its completion in time for the 1935-36 season. Other help came from the Depression-born Civilian Conservation Corps which cleared trees for new runs.

Dr. Joel Hildebrand

Alex Hildebrand

THE SKIING HILDEBRANDS

As pioneering ski families go, the late Dr. Joel and Emily Hildebrand and their clan were tough to beat.

In 1930-31, the entire Hildebrand family spent a year in Switzerland. They took lessons from the famed Hannes Schneider at his world-famous ski school in St. Anton, Austria. After returning to Berkeley, they shared their newfound knowledge and skill with others by teaching, coaching and giving advice on equipment.

During the ensuing years, the children, Alex, Milton, Roger and Louise, were strong competitors on the ski slopes.

In December 1932, skiing for the University of California at Berkeley, Alex won the first intercollegiate cross-country race in Yosemite Valley by more than ten minutes. A year later in the first Winter Club race on the newly opened slopes at Badger Pass, the Hildebrand team came home with four medals. Alex and Louise took gold, eleven-year-old Roger a silver, and fifteen-year-old Milton a bronze medal. Milton and Roger followed Alex to Cal

where they, too, joined the ski team.

After their year in Europe, however, Emily Hildebrand chose to stay home and provide logistical support for her traveling family. Dr. Hildebrand explained her decision, "Mrs. Hildebrand has decided to retire on her laurels and to be the only 'sane' member of the Hildebrand family."

In 1936, Dr. Hildebrand managed the American ski team at the Fourth Winter Olympics at Garmisch, Germany. His specialty was setting slalom races, and later he was often called upon to set courses at major ski meets.

"We didn't believe our skiing prowess was so great . . . The competition in those days was sparse and the equipment poor by today's standards," recalled a modest Alex Hildebrand in 1998.

The Hildebrands were emissaries of American skiing and today their grandchildren continue the family tradition of seeking the magic of winters everywhere.

*Yosemite's new Tyrolean Ski House opened
in December 1935 to a foot of fresh snow.
A week-long series of activities in Yosemite Valley
centered around the festive Winter Sports Carnival
at the Ahwahnee and Curry Village skating rink.
The lodge's dedication on January 5, 1936,
offered testimony to Tresidder's significant
commitment to making Badger Pass a mecca
for ski sports. The pageantry culminated
at the ski area with the coronation of popular Yosemite
siblings Jack and Helen Patterson
as the carnival's king and queen.*

Badger Pass now provided skiers with one of the finest ski lodges in North America. The building, designed by E. T. Spencer of San Francisco who also built the Snow Creek ski cabin, offered a wide array of amenities and service, including indoor plumbing, appreciated by all who had exposed themselves to the cold the previous seasons.

The best improvement of all, however, was the addition of large sleds that carried eight standing passengers at a time to the top of Granite Dome, replacing the temporary contraption of the year before. Christened the "Up-ski" or "Queen Mary," in honor of Mary Tresidder, it was the first of its kind in the West. The two sleds, counterbalanced and pulled by a three-eighths-inch cable, moved uphill a distance of 1,850 feet to an elevation 600 feet above the new lodge. When running full bore, the lift had a capacity of one hundred skiers an hour.

Loading the "Queen Mary," twin sleds pulled by a cable.

Arguably, the 1935-36 ski season's most significant addition at Badger Pass occurred with the arrival of twenty-six-year-old Hannes Schroll. Flamboyant, handsome and athletic, the dynamic Austrian joined the Yosemite Ski School as director. In April, Hannes had won both the slalom and downhill events at the Nationals at Mount Rainier, Washington. Eight thousand spectators, including Don and Mary Tresidder, watched Schroll laugh and yodel his way down the fog-covered courses. He won the slalom by 12.3 seconds and finished the downhill an unbelievable 1.7 minutes ahead of his nearest rival, Dick Durrance of Dartmouth. *The Seattle Post-Intelligencer* reported on Schroll's run, "As his blades struck a drift, the impetus sent him flying through the air an estimated sixty feet. Keeping perfect control of his skis in some amazing fashion, he maneuvered back into safe terrain and went yodeling on his merry way to victory."

Winner of more than one hundred international ski titles in Europe, Schroll came from the small southern Tyrolean hamlet of Konguehue where he took his first

In his Waco airplane, Don Tresidder delivered the new director of the Yosemite Ski School, Hannes Schroll, to Wawona from San Francisco.

Watching a race at Badger Pass, circa 1937.
Don Tresidder is on the left, Hannes Schroll and Wolfgang Lert,
racer and coach of UCLA's ski team, are on the right.
The identity of the other two is unknown.

lesson as a boy of four under the watchful eye of his father. In 1934 he captured the hazardous Marmolata Race in the Italian Alps, known throughout ski circles as the fastest downhill in the world. It was dictator Benito Mussolini who presented Hannes with his trophy ring. More importantly, the win earned Schroll a ticket to the races at Mount Rainier and he never returned to teach in his troubled homeland.

Lured by the Tresidders to Yosemite, Schroll replaced veteran Jules Fritsch who stayed on as his assistant. Fritsch was a cross-country skier at heart; Hannes loved alpine skiing above all else. Colorful and romantic, he embodied a sense of the dramatic. Godlike in ability, the heavily accented Schroll was also a social person who truly enjoyed teaching guests how to ski and partying with them at the end of the day.

"Hannes Schroll, newly appointed director of the Yosemite Ski School, announced the opening of his classes on December 20th. Not only is Schroll one of the world's greatest skiers—holding the American Downhill and

Slalom Championships as well as the Austrian titles—he is a fine and experienced instructor. His school in Austria was one of the largest and best in Europe," the Yosemite Park & Curry Company proclaimed enthusiastically.

His dashing and daring style hit Yosemite skiing like an avalanche. A wave of skiers, from entry level to advanced, lined up for his school, flocking to Badger Pass to meet the "Red Devil of Tyrol."

Winter sports director Jimmy Connell capitalized on the new director's notoriety by regularly sending Hannes to San Francisco to promote skiing at Badger Pass. Bill Klein, a fellow Austrian who headed the ski school at the Sierra Club's Clair Tappaan lodge at Donner Summit, remembers one such trip. "I stayed with him at the Mark Hopkins. Hannes loved cars. He had a Ford and I didn't have a car. He had to go to a meeting and told me to take the car and pick him up near the Ferry Building. And so I get the car out of the garage and drive down California Street. It's quite steep so I start using the brakes, and there are no brakes in the car! I use low gear

and the hand brake and go through Montgomery street, past a policeman directing traffic telling me to stop. I finally come to a stop in the middle of the street. He let me go because I guess I didn't speak English. I got to Hannes and he said, 'I forgot to tell you the brakes don't work too good!' This was typical Hannes."

Even with the installation of the Up-ski, Bill Cahow, a future ski instructor from Fresno, continued to hike for his turns, unable to afford the twenty-five cents per ride. This didn't detract from his enthusiasm. He remembers that Badger's blend of trails and open-slope skiing helped revolutionize the sport. "For a young kid, it was the most exciting time of my life. While the skiing was primitive to what would come along later, it was still an adventure. Just being there was an adventure."

As marvelous as the Up-ski was, the lift battled many mechanical problems. Its carriage could not operate readily in deep or fresh snow. It often broke down. Despite the difficulties and a limited rider capacity, the Up-ski provided modern transportation to increasing numbers of skiers.

Step right up and get your lessons from Jules Fritsch, Hannes Schroll, Gordon Hooley and Ralph de Pfyffer, the 1935-36 ski school staff.

You can almost hear Hannes saying, "Bend your knees young lady, bend your knees!"

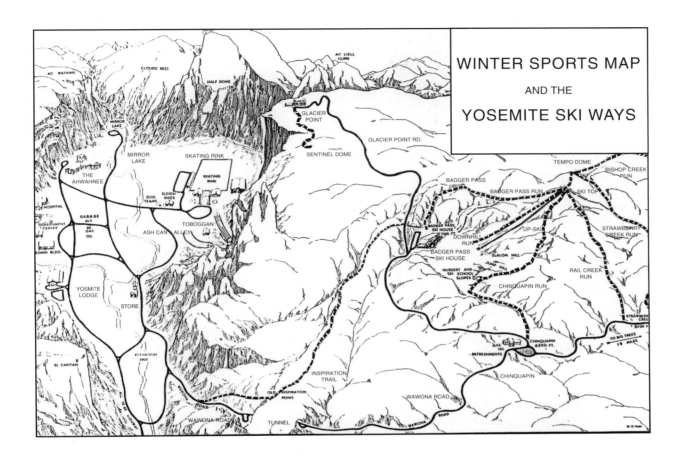

WINTER SPORTS MAP

AND THE

YOSEMITE SKI WAYS

"These trails gave rise to some good skiing and ski stories," Bill Cahow recalled. "There was a seldom used cross-over trail known as 'Railberry' that started on Rail Creek and ended on Strawberry Creek. One day a few of us detoured off that way and we came upon a couple in a rather embarrassing, non-skiing position."

The ski trails that began at Badger Pass added immensely to its popularity. The long, gentle Chinquapin run quickly gained the reputation as a "snowplow special." *Ski High In Yosemite*, a company guidebook, noted that only the Badger Pass and Chinquapin runs offered beginner terrain. "The Chinquapin run is a true test for 'stemming' for the trail is too narrow to permit Christianias. In late afternoon, when the run becomes a bit iced, even professionals can thrill to the speed of its course." Its great popularity certainly had something to do with the ski hut at the end of the run where skiers gathered to meet friends over a hot drink and food.

For experts, the longest and hardest run was the Inspiration Trail, also called the Bridalvail Trail. Its advanced terrain dropped 4,000 feet in ten miles to Yosemite Valley via Old Inspiration Point and the old Wawona

Road. "A perfect day of skiing can be spent here, in view of Yosemite Valley and the High Sierra," read the guidebook. However, it also noted, "This cross-country trip should not be attempted without a guide."

The Bishop Creek, Rail Creek and Strawberry Creek Trails plunged down the back side of Badger Pass over slopes logged years before the area became part of the park. Each trail dropped over 2,000 feet in two to three miles, terminating at the Wawona Road. Unfortunately, these south-facing runs offered inconsistent snow. Surface conditions, often great at the top, tended to be patchy or even bare near the bottom. Still, Rail Creek, with its 2,500-foot vertical and tricky transitions, became the site for many major downhill ski events.

*Although accommodations for overnight stays were not available,
the Ski House offered almost every other convenience—
ski waxing and locker rooms, a ski rental department,
cafeteria and comfortable lounge with
a large open fireplace for weary skiers.
The broad terrace quickly became the favorite spot
for guests to lunch or wax skis, bask in the sun,
and watch the activities on the slopes.*

*Miss Australia, Peggy Gamble, was
chosen to represent her country at the
1936 Tournament of Roses
in Pasadena, California.
What better way to cap
that triumph than to visit Badger Pass
for a private lesson with Hannes Schroll.*

TWO GREAT YOSEMITE SKIERS

Tom Sovulewski winning an interclub slalom in 1936.

Tom Sovulewski and his sister Gabe Goldsworthy were two of Yosemite's best skiers. Their father Gabriel was the first civilian park supervisor. As a young man Tom worked for the National Park Service building trails and fighting fires. He moved to Fresno just before World War II, where he was a member and coach of the Fresno Ski Club. Later he worked as a general contractor. Gabe was a thoroughly modern woman, a good horsewoman and a great hiker who loved the mountains. She was elected several times as Mariposa County Clerk after the war.

Gabe Goldsworthy with Hannes Schroll.

The friendly ambiance had the marketing office trumpeting, "At Badger Pass you can ski in comfort, warmed by the winter sun and protected from cold winds. Weather conditions are comparable to those found in the most favored ski areas in Switzerland, and skiing is usually good from December to May."

Almost any weekend of the winter season, visitors found a full series of events. When no major competition was scheduled, winter sports director Jimmy Connell offered guests recreational activities such as the Sunday Slalom Races, the Gold and Silver Ski Tests and ski school classes.

Badger Pass was beginning to attract the world's greatest skiers. The Auburn Ski Club's Roy Mikkelsen practiced at Badger Pass for the 1936 Winter Olympic Games in Garmisch, Germany. In February 1936, the resort hosted the expanded Pacific Coast Intercollegiate Skiing Championships. The Huskies of the University of Washington outclassed the other western schools. "Almost fifty men competed for the ten teams, making it the largest college ski meet ever to be held on the Pacific Coast. Most of the events were run in a driving snow storm which kept the course in fine shape and added many feet of new snow to the slopes," the *Yosemite Ski News* reported.

By the end of the new lodge's first season, ski lessons were up forty percent. Skier days had nearly tripled from 12,000 to 31,600.

The park might not have won its bid for the 1932 Winter Olympic Games but its winter sports program had helped make Yosemite one of the country's finest year-round destinations. The Yosemite Winter Club was established, as well as the first ski school in the West. Yosemite had helped found the powerful California Ski Association. The Ahwahnee Hotel and its Bracebridge pageant were known worldwide. The National Park Service had gained a strong foothold in Washington with Yosemite as its benchmark program. Don Tresidder had much to be proud of.

For a comparatively brief period before the Second World War,
Badger Pass stood at the top as the foremost ski area in the nation.
Its ski school, in particular, was world renowned.

KING OF THE HILL
1936 - 1941

I n California, alpine skiing was emerging from almost complete obscurity to front-page news. With its well-organized sports club and strong development of winter programs, Yosemite was the center of activity for the ski-crazed West. Badger Pass's popularity was filling hotel rooms in the Valley.

In 1936, with facilities unmatched at any other area and led by one of the foremost skiers in the world, Yosemite stood at the top of American winter sports. To spread the word, Tresidder added Ansel Adams and David Brower to the publicity department. The talented pair, future leaders of the environmental movement in America, added punch to Yosemite's marketing efforts. Both were accomplished skiers. Brower, only twenty-six, had made the first winter ascents of Mount Lyell and Mount Clark. They released grand photos and glowing news reports.

As the thirties advanced, so too did ski instruction. Badger Pass arguably had the best ski school in the country, especially after Sigi Engl arrived from Austria to join Hannes Schroll for the 1936-37 season. A two-time Austrian ski champion, Engl had also been champion of Italy and France, and a recent winner of the famous Marmolata downhill. Bill Cahow remembered Sigi as a superior skier and instructor. "His style was superb; he could ski as smooth as anyone I had ever seen. He had personal skills that were more effective—he was a better communicator and a better teacher than Hannes." Engl would capture the first Far West Kandahar and the 1941 National Open Slalom at Yosemite. He also won Sun Valley's

"Yosemite ski life centers about the picturesque Badger Pass Ski House, which is located in a sheltered mountain meadow at 7,300 feet elevation. In less than 45 minutes from the time you leave the Ahwahnee or Yosemite Lodge you can be driving into the spacious parking area at Badger," heralded the advertising brochures.

Harriman Cup in 1940, executing a casual Geländesprung in the finish corral. Engl was elected to the U.S. National Ski Hall of Fame in 1971.

Don Tresidder became a vice-president of the California Ski Association and used his influence to host numerous and important ski races. The California Downhill and Slalom Championships were held at Badger Pass in March 1937. Yosemite's Tom Sovulewski, Leroy Rust and Bill Stark finished third, fourth and fifth behind Sig Ulland of the Lake Tahoe Ski Club. Gabe Goldsworthy was the women's champion.

The following year the Civilian Conservation Corps built a thirty-meter ski jump at Badger. Now all the ski disciplines—jumping, cross-country, slalom and downhill—could be contested in one meet. At the 1938 Pacific Coast Intercollegiate Championships, Carl Bechdolt of the University of Nevada won Yosemite's first jumping competition. Ninety-six entrants from sixteen colleges competed overall, making the championships the largest ski meet ever held in Yosemite National Park. The Far West Kandahar, the B. Charles Ehrman Trophy

Photograph by David Brower

Sigi Engl performing a Geländesprung off a snow-covered rock at Badger Pass.

Race, the California Inter-Club Meet, the Wilbur May Challenge Trophy, the Dodge Trophy Race and other prestigious races filled the schedule.

In 1936, when Mary and Don Tresidder returned to Europe, they had visited St. Anton, Austria, where they met Hannes Schneider, founder of the Arlberg ski school,

and known in every alpine country as the father of modern skiing. Few sportsmen commanded the respect that Schneider generated. His ski school, started in 1922 at the Hotel Post, was the most prestigious in the world and had helped make St. Anton a skiers mecca. Children, students, wealthy socialites and sports-minded royalty all traveled

there to learn to ski under his tutelage. When Schneider roared, "Knie beugen!" even kings bent their knees. In 1930, he was invited to Japan where he taught six classes a day, each with five hundred students.

The Tresidders tried to lure Schneider to teach at Yosemite. The famed instructor, whose students in St. Anton included the Duke of Hamilton, Prince Nicholas of Rumania, famed Italian race car driver Piero Taruffi, King Albert of Belgium and actress Claudette Colbert, politely declined.

However, some of Schneider's most promising pupils had developed into a strong instructors' corps. Sigi Engl was one of his instructors. Others who would go on to fame in the United States included Toni Matt, Otto Lang, Friedl Pfeifer and Benno Rybizka.

The Tresidders were introduced to Luggi Foeger who, according to fellow skier Otto Lang, "was unquestionably the star among the instructors." Born April 21, 1907, in Austria's western state of Tyrol, Luggi was an authoritative figure who had already spent twelve years working under Schneider's strict eye. He had taught and become close friends with Jerome Hill, son of the builder of the Great Northern Railway and whose family skied at Yosemite. The German-speaking Hill, a graduate of Yale studying in Paris, taught Luggi to speak English.

The Tresidders were impressed with the brown-haired, blue-eyed Austrian who appeared so lithe and supple on skis. They marveled at his teaching methods and technical refinement. They offered to arrange for Luggi's immigration and extended him an invitation to settle in Yosemite. It was not until two years later in 1938, with the decline of tourism and skiing in the Arlberg as a result of Hitler's rise, that Foeger decided to leave his boyhood slopes to come to Badger Pass.

It was a momentous decision for the thirty-one-year-old. Shortly after his departure from his homeland in March, the Anschluss swept over Austria. His mentor Hannes Schneider was jailed by the Nazis and only through the efforts of high-placed friends would he be able to arrange transit

Luggi Foeger.

*"Luggi was so good with people. He really understood
the needs of the individual," says Jurgen Wetzstein,
a ski instructor from Immenstadt, Germany, who taught for Foeger.
"But sometimes he was hard on people, too.
I remember him asking a husband he discovered on the slope
trying to teach his wife incorrectly how to ski, 'Sir, why don't you use a
sledgehammer on her if you're trying to kill her?
It is the only right thing to do and much quicker.'"*

to America in 1939 to avoid a war-torn Europe.

Luggi's arrival at Yosemite in 1938 coincided with the departure of both Sigi Engl and Hannes Schroll and the arrival of Charley Proctor. Engl left to open a ski school on Conway Summit before moving on to Sun Valley. The twenty-eight-year-old Schroll devoted himself to establishing the Sugar Bowl resort on Donner Summit. "Hannes was a great skier, but he was also very loud and at times outspoken or verbally abrasive," recalled Bill Cahow. Bill remembered that on more than one occasion Schroll offended the sedate Mary Tresidder with comments that were not always well received. "I think it had something to do with her skiing—and telling her to keep her ass down. In his last year, I think Schroll was at the point where he was about to be fired, but he didn't care," says Cahow.

"Hannes loved Yosemite. Of course, he was treated royally. He was well-liked," recalls Bill Klein. It was Klein who helped Schroll conceive of Sugar Bowl after introducing him to the Donner Summit area. "But Hannes also had a very natural personality. He said what he thought and acted as he wanted. I think he had bigger dreams than what Yosemite offered him after a while."

Luggi Foeger displayed a warm, disarming personality that radiated easily across national boundaries. Yet, for all his charm and smiles, he was at times self-centered. He was eager to put his stamp on his new world. Adapting the Arlberg technique, which his mentor Hannes Schneider had invented, Luggi developed a teaching method that included not just one, but numerous turns, all linked together in a continuous flow. As he wrote in the *Yosemite Winter Club Year Book* for 1941-42, "Turns are built one on top of the other and the perfect whole is a stem christiania."

With the goal "to teach people how to ski with ease and grace," Luggi's success at Badger Pass gained him as strong a following as he had had in St. Anton. Publicist Ben Tarnutzer wrote, "He established a uniform method of instruction throughout the various classes so pupils are not confused as they progress from one class to another."

The Ski School in 1938-39. Front row: Charley Proctor, Jules Fritsch and Tyler Micoleau.
Back row: Luggi Foeger, Gordon Hooley, Ralph de Pfyffer and Jack Patterson.

Like Hannes Schneider, Foeger had a gift for recruiting a cadre of top instructors into his ski school.
During the late 1930s, legendary skiers Tyler Micoleau, Jack Patterson, Bob Skinner, Arnold Fawcus,
Gabe Goldsworthy and Marshall Fitzgerald all taught under his watchful eye.
He was committed to keeping the standards of his instructors as high as possible.
As he implored, "Set the example for your students. Dress correctly, use the correct equipment,
and conduct yourselves with the highest standard of courtesy."

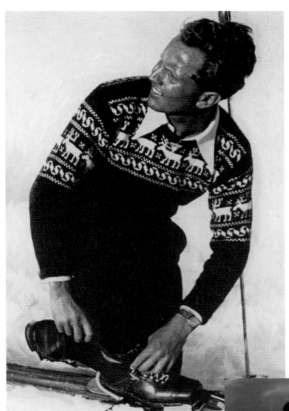

Luggi and Helen Foeger

"Luggi ran a good ski school. Everyone respected him. All the guys wanted to work for Luggi," recalls Bill Klein. "There was good opportunity staying with Luggi." One of his assistants, Helen Henderson, made the most of working with the handsome skimeister. The two married on June 18, 1943.

Luggi was not without a great sense of humor. Invited to dine with his students who stayed at the Ahwahnee, he found the hotel's dining room to be "like a church, too quiet and stuffy where everyone tiptoed around." He demanded that weekly specials be offered to guests along with weekend dinner dances. "You wouldn't believe what a business all of a sudden it was. It wasn't a church anymore!"

"I remember one particular race in 1939," says Bill Klein. "There were a lot of Austrians, of course, at the banquet. They had a few drinks before dinner already and they began climbing the walls of the Ahwahnee. They have these river rock walls the fellows climbed to the top. I don't remember if Luggi made it to the top, but it got a little out of hand. It looked like a bunch of monkeys crawling around."

For all its popularity, learning to ski didn't arrive without a price. Schussing down slopes of breakable crust without a modicum of control and only a prayer on the lips resulted in punishing falls. Most Californians, much like today, were forced to confine their skiing to weekend

trips and consequently had little opportunity to get into shape. Novices taking up the sport for the first time easily exhausted themselves, sometimes just gathering their equipment in the parking lot! Given the soft leather boots, loose and ineffective toe-iron and bear-trap bindings, and long unwieldy wooden skis, broken ankles and other fractures were not uncommon. Without an organized ski patrol, the ski instructor became the on-slope doctor.

"A broken leg was worth big money to the Depression-plagued hospital. The x-ray, setting, casting and an overnight stay cost $100 in those days," recalled Dr. Avery Sturm, a physician at Yosemite's Lewis Memorial Hospital. Viewing such firsthand accidents did not deter Sturm from getting caught up in the sport. "I became an avid skier, loved every moment of it and only ended up in plaster once."

Fresno skier Franklin Knapp recalled that on his first trip to Yosemite in the early 1930s he saw people skiing in old working boots nailed to barrel staves. Or they were on homemade skis, hewn from $1.50 ski blanks of maple or hickory. By the late 1930s, everyone was on manufactured skis, the best of which cost about $25 dollars. At Montgomery Ward a complete ski outfit could be bought for less than $15. The ski boots were big and clumsy with little or no support. The toe-release bindings, invented by Mount Hood's Hjalmar Hvam, arrived in 1937. "Everything was experimental, but there was a lot of fun and pioneering spirit," Knapp reminisced years later.

Wolfgang Lert, a racer and coach for UCLA's ski team in the 1930s, remembers a collegiate race at Yosemite that typified the danger of those days.

"I was coaching the UCLA team. The downhill course went down Rail Creek. We had lots of heavy new snow, and the courses were not well-prepared," says Lert. "I complained to Luggi who bawled me out as being a sissy and told me to shut up." The UCLA team began training on Rail Creek where an unexpected switchback fooled everyone. The whole team including the coach shot off the course into the bushes and brambles.

Skiers at Badger Pass in the mid 1930s.

"I ended upside down with my legs hung up in some branches, and groaning with a painful ankle," Lert recalls sixty years later. "Suddenly I heard another groan below me. 'Please get off my head, Wolfgang.' One of my racers was also upside down, with his head buried in the snow. I had skied over his chin, nicking it ever so slightly with my edge."

In pain, Lert struggled gingerly to his feet. With his ankle still tightly laced inside its boot, he slowly and haltingly negotiated the remainder of the course to his car. He sat out the rest of the ski season with a cast on his leg.

Don Tresidder had an eye for ski talent. He often looked abroad for skilled professionals who would help make Yosemite the foremost ski area in North America.

But that changed when he found Charley Proctor, a somewhat reserved eastern skier who made his mark while still a student at Dartmouth College in New Hampshire. Proctor was one of the first and best American-born skiers.

Exposed to skiing as a four-year-old in his native New Hampshire, Proctor went on to captain the Dartmouth ski team in 1927. That year he won the Nordic Combined Championship of Canada. He competed in cross-country skiing and jumping at the 1928 Winter Olympics Games at St. Moritz, Switzerland. (There were no alpine events that year.) Between 1935 and 1937, he coached the Harvard Ski Team and authored several books on skiing, including *Skiing—Fundamental Equipment and Advanced Technique*, which became a bible for early skiers.

Proctor often spoke about the strange reaction he got in the early 1920s when he carried his eight-foot-long skis through the train stations along the East Coast. "It was a rather unusual sight. At that time there were only a handful of us doing it, skiing, which was mainly cross-countrying and jumping. Very few people knew anything about skis or skiing," he recalled.

On a western business trip in 1932, Proctor met the dynamic Don Tresidder, and the two skied together on the slopes of Badger. Before the day was over, Proctor had been offered the job as Yosemite's winter sports director but it would take until 1938 before Tresidder could convince Charley to come west to stay.

Proctor plunged into his new job like a racer out of the starting gate. He worked with the Tresidders to upgrade the lifts, runs and ice rink to make Yosemite a destination ski area and resort. Through the years, Proctor served skiing in numerous capacities, always seeking to advance his beloved sport.

For his dedication Proctor was inducted into the U.S. National Ski Hall of Fame in 1959. A year later he served on the Olympic Ski Advisory Committee for the 1960 Squaw Valley Winter Games. Proctor skied on and on, finally retiring in 1971—his love affair with Yosemite and skiing as strong and enduring as ever.

The "Charley Proctor Award" has been given annually since 1981 by the western division of the North American Ski Journalists Association to an individual who has contributed significantly to the sport of skiing, a fitting tribute to the man who was at the forefront of American skiing for more than four decades.

"It's been a great life, working and skiing in one of the most beautiful places in America," he said. Proctor passed away in 1996.

Charley Proctor wearing his trademark cap, circa 1940.

Courtesy of Jane Rust

49

Badger Pass played host to many important races during the 1938-39 ski season, claiming California's most complete winter program. War raged throughout Europe and Asia, but Yosemite remained a separate world, isolated from the chaotic, fear-ridden times. If anything, Yosemite was an antidote for many visitors to the horrors abroad. The beautiful ski fields surrounded by forests of Sierra conifer and hedges of Alpine buckwheat allowed them to escape the real world and enter another. Three years later, Pearl Harbor would shatter everyone's lives and change the ski world forever.

In March 1939, Badger Pass hosted the Pacific Coast Intercollegiate Ski Championships. Nearly two hundred racers from nineteen schools competed. Seventy competitors raced in the downhill, hurtling along Rail Creek in one-minute intervals. From Ski Top to the old railroad grade, three pairs of gates on the Big Hill forced the skiers to make controlled high-speed turns. Because of interval starts and the complete lack of communication with gatekeepers, some of the athletes were overtaken by faster

competitors. Sixty-eight racers managed to finish, even though two or three appeared to get lost or confused along the way. Race times varied. Fresno's Dick Mitchell, a member of the University of Nevada ski team, was first at three minutes, six seconds, while it took a University of Oregon racer over fifteen minutes to finish.

Mitchell also won the slalom. Bob Barto of the University of Washington bested the field of cross-country skiers. Although Dave Quinney of Utah captured the jumping competition, Tom Murstad, a visiting jumper from Norway, won the admiration of the crowd. Flying off the lip of the ski jump on Badger Hill, he completed a midair somersault, much to the amazement of the large crowd of onlookers.

Later in the season, Yosemite welcomed the inaugural Far West Kandahar. Cosponsored by the Yosemite Winter Club and the Sierra Club, the races were sanctioned by the California Ski Association. Patterned after the famous Arlberg-Kandahar of Austria, it attracted some of the world's greatest racers. Before the war, the Far West Kandahar

Sigi Engl displaying the style that made him a great teacher and racer.

alternated between Yosemite and Mount Hood, Oregon.

Future Badger Pass instructor Bill Cahow remembered the Kandahar as "big time ski races." Large crowds of skiers lined the race course and packed the finishing corrals. A short, demanding downhill course was set over soft spring-like conditions along the long twisting Rail Creek trail. Every sixty seconds a competitor dropped into the 1.9 mile course that featured a steep drop off a cornice, then hung on through trees onto a rocky nose that resulted in several spectacular spills and broken skis. Sigi Engl, then with the Mono Ski Club, finished first, followed by Fred Iselin of France and Yosemite's own Luggi Foeger and Leroy Rust.

Luggi set Saturday's slalom race on the Big Hill, a tight course of thirty-two gates. The weather turned colder which hardened the snow into a fast surface. Engl once again dominated, winning the slalom and capturing the combined title. Iselin, Foeger and Rust rounded out the top four in the combined.

In the women's competition, Clarita Heath, a fast-rising new racer from the Mono Ski Club and member of the 1936 United States Ski Team at the Garmisch Olympics, swept both the downhill and the slalom to win the combined title. Yosemite racers Gabe Goldsworthy and Mary Proctor finished fourth and sixth.

Clarita Heath and Sigi Engl, winners at the first Far West Kandahar.

CLARITA HEATH

This excerpt from the *Western Skier* in March 1937 says it all:

"The girl who is making Europe take notice of American skiers, Miss Clarita Heath of Pasadena, entered the annual Arlberg-Kandahar ski races held in the Austrian Alps on March 6 and 7. She represented the Yosemite Winter Club.

"Miss Heath first came to prominence in European ski centers when she took two second places in the Swiss championships held at Les Diablerets. . . . A week later, in the FIS meet held at Chamonix, France, when pitted against the world's best woman skiers, she placed fourth in the straight race and 13th in the slalom. This is by far the best any American skier has done in international competitions of this calibre.

"Miss Heath's performance is even more amazing when it is realized that she has been skiing only two years. . . .

"She took her first lessons at Kitzbuhel, Austria, from Siegfried Engl, who is now one of the top instructors in the Yosemite Ski School. . . ."

A week after the Arlberg-Kandahar, a first in the downhill and a second in the slalom gave Clarita the combined championship in the Austrian women's competition.

Clarita Heath Bright was elected to the U.S. National Ski Hall of Fame in 1968.

In twenty sixth place that day, Dave McCoy of the Eastern Sierra Ski Club, was hardly noticed. Yet within two years this ski pioneer would become a formidable racer, winning the California State Championship in 1941. Injuries eventually forced his retirement from racing, but not from influencing future generations of skiers. During the 1950s and 1960s, the developer of Mammoth Mountain coached many racers onto the United States Ski Team, including Jill Kinmont and his daughter Penny McCoy.

Two other racers ran into trouble of their own making that weekend. In the midst of opening the Sugar Bowl Resort, Hannes Schroll returned to Yosemite in time for the Kandahar.

"Luggi was the course setter," recalls Bill Klein, who entered under the banner of the Sierra Club. "Most of us were there a couple days early skiing in the Valley, but Hannes came on Friday. He comes to me and says he wants to look at the course. I say, 'Hannes, the course is closed. You're not allowed to go on the course.' He knew the regulations, but the next thing I know we are

skiing down off to the side and Hannes drifts into the course. There are a bunch of guys, including Charley Proctor and Luggi, working on it. Luggi immediately gets upset. 'What are you doing!' he screams. Of course we weren't supposed to do what we'd done, but we kept going."

Schroll finished first on Saturday in the downhill only to have his results thrown out the following morning. "That was a mistake by the committee. They should have disqualified us immediately," says Klein whose fifth place finish in the downhill was also stricken from the results. "Instead, they didn't tell us until we were on top of the slalom course the next day preparing to race."

Hannes didn't take his banishment kindly. "He was really upset. He tore off his number and schussed straight down the hill right through the slalom course," remembers Bill. "I thought 'what the hell' and raced and came in second in the slalom. It would have given me the second in the combined if I hadn't been disqualified. I didn't blame Luggi; it was our fault."

Looking out at the Ski Hill in 1938.

Courtesy of Jane Rust

Leroy Rust, circa 1940.

Charley Proctor on Horse Ridge in 1941.

At the end of March 1939, the Yosemite ski team traveled to Mammoth Mountain on the eastern slope of the Sierra for the California State Championships. Hosts included Dave McCoy and his wife Roma, active members of the Mammoth Mountain Ski Club and Winter Sports Association. McCoy had established his first rope tow at Deadman's Summit, just north of the town of Mammoth Lakes. By 1941 he would set up a rope tow on Mammoth Mountain and open the resort after the war. In 1939, however, there were no lifts, lodges or groomed runs to greet the racers—only open, snow-laden slopes surrounded by majestic primeval beauty. The competitors were handed a sack lunch as they climbed to the starting gate on the upper slopes. The thrilling 2,000-foot downhill course was marked by only start and finish gates. "It was 'down mountain' racing, as skiing was meant to be," said one competitor.

The slalom was held the following day in the face of a mounting snowstorm. A forty-mile-per-hour gale whipped up particles of ice that blinded racers. The weather numbed spectators and drove over two-thirds of the field from the course. "It was impossible to see up the course because of the sleet and wind, and the men in charge of the gates got behind trees and watched the skiers as they went by. The wind had blown all the loose snow off the course and left an icy pack. Several skiers found the wind and cold not to their liking and did not take a second run," observed the Winter Club annual.

Adverse conditions didn't stop the skiing elder statesman from Auburn Ski Club, Roy Mikkelsen, from capturing the combined. The thirty-two-year-old Norwegian was far from intimidated by his younger counterparts. In twelve years competing in jumping, downhill and slalom the two-time Olympian had compiled twenty-seven club championships, fifteen state titles and two national championships.

The Yosemite female contingent, Gabe Goldsworthy, Mary Proctor and Lisa Adams, swept the field. A disappointed Yosemite men's squad was lead by Leroy Rust who finished a distant seventh.

In 1936, Sun Valley, Idaho, had opened with fanfare. Its chairlift, the nation's first, quickly captured the attention of those who could afford to ski in style. By the end of the decade, new resorts were blossoming at Alta in Utah, Aspen in Colorado, and Mount Hood in Oregon. At Donner Summit, Hannes Schroll was drawing skiers to the superb, lift-accessed runs of Sugar Bowl. Badger Pass still had an advantage because of its close proximity to urban populations in California, and, of course, Yosemite's incomparable beauty. Hollywood stars and other celebrities enjoyed the grandeur of the Ahwahnee and the pristine slopes of Badger Pass, lending their glitter to the unfolding ski scene. Douglas Fairbanks, Andy Devine, Norma Shearer, Jon Garfield and other stars were close on the heels of Charlie Chaplin to the slopes.

Madeline Carroll added her fair share of notoriety to Yosemite's glamorous personalities. The blonde bombshell reigned as one of Hollywood's foremost stars and sex symbols, and with good reason. More than a few Winter Club members crashed trying to catch a glimpse of the queen of film learning to ski.

Ski Top at Badger Pass.

Bringing in an injured skier.

After creation of the National Ski Patrol in 1938,
Don Tresidder became the divisional chairman for California.
Until then, response to ski accidents fell into the laps of park rangers
and any company employees who could be mustered.
In the winter of 1939-40, there were 126 injured skiers
at Badger Pass, fifty-four with fractures or dislocations.

"During the first weekend of skiing at Badger [in December 1939], those present were treated to the lovely image of Madeline Carroll—sans klieg lights, sans makeup, sans complete self control—doing her level best to assimilate the teachings of Ralph de Pfyffer, most patient member of Yosemite's fine staff of ski instructors. All of which would seem to be official confirmation of the ever increasing popularity of skiing among celebrities," the Fresno Ski Club's *Skiesta News* reported January 3, 1940.

Sixty thousand skiers visited Badger Pass during the 1939-40 season. Improvements and added facilities helped accommodate the sometimes overwhelming crowds. The park service had resurfaced the highway from Chinquapin to Badger Pass. Ski slopes and trails were improved. By the early 1940s, four parallel sleds of the Up-ski carried passengers up the Big Hill. "There was a long line of Up-skis," remembers Nadine Malm Powers of the Stanford Ski Club. "There was one known as Big Bertha. Another was called the Normandie. They got us to the top of the hill, but the wait at times became excessive."

Long lines didn't detract from the fun of Fresno native and ten-year-old Larry Huebner. "Badger Pass was about the only ski area in the state with an Up-ski. We thought it was fantastic. An all-day ticket was a dollar, but you could get a single ride for 25 cents. Our family would get the single ride and then ski out to Tempo Dome. Most of our skiing was climbing, but we would go up and down the dome. There was no groomed snow or anything like that. Often it was junk snow. We groomed the run by boot-packing," he recollects.

A good skier might get only two or three rides on the Up-ski on a crowded day. As lift lines stretched longer, enduring waits became more difficult, eventually leading to some frustration and occasional snowball exchanges. The high jinks prompted the editor of the *Skiesta News* to toss his own verbal missile in the February 28, 1941, issue. "Yosemite should do something about those funny people that throw snowballs on the Up-ski," he quipped in print. "There is a park rule that says you can't throw anything at any moving objects, and if it is true that violators are subject to a $5

The new rope tows were a welcome addition in 1940.

fine, then we were unfortunate enough to pass one Up-ski (coming down) that was carrying about $180 worth of potential misdemeanors." A subsequent edition accused some skiers of riding both ways on the Up-ski, unable to face the challenge of the hill.

Frustrated crowds were pacified with the addition of two rope tows in the fall of 1940. Both 1,000 feet in length, one was installed to the right of the Jump Hill and the other between the top of the Up-ski and Temple Dome. Rope tows were quite common throughout the state by that time. In fact, more than sixty-five gave access to Sierra ski slopes. Their late introduction to Yosemite, however, brought mixed reactions, if not apprehension. While they improved the uphill capacity, they also inflicted a certain amount of pain and confusion on inexperienced users.

"Never flirt with a rope tow until you have been properly introduced," wryly advised Yosemite publicist Ben Tarnutzer. "I will never forget those first few days at Badger when our two rope tows, each about a half-mile in length, were put in operation. Every minute or two the tows had to be stopped while some prostrate skier, either by his own frantic efforts or with the help of whoever happened to be near, struggled to extricate himself from a pretzel-like position that was usually as embarrassing as it was uncomfortable."

Even some of Yosemite's better skiers had their humiliating moments. Gabe Goldsworthy managed to "learn the ropes" by securing guidance from the strong arm of Charley Proctor. "If you know the ropes you can get a lot more fun out of your skiing. The first few days the rope tows were operating, I kept at what I felt was a safe distance from this entangling, endless serpent, ever winding upward... [Later] I was clinging to the rope with my vocal chords as well as all the new muscles I could muster in my wrists. 'Help! Transfer here.' And somehow I made it to the top," Gabe reported.

Emulating Proctor, the prudent skier soon acquired a "rope-tow gripper," a large alligator clip that resembled a nutcracker and saved a lot of aching arm muscles.

Skiers on Sentinel Dome in 1941 as movie cameras recorded the action.

Tarnutzer noted that compared to the Up-ski, the rope tows were lightning fast. One eager skier claimed ten round trips in an hour. The *Skiesta News* of January 3, 1940, gave a rave review. "Last Sunday at Yosemite was a 'super-duper,' ... Three feet of perfect packed snow and the rope tow for all day for a dollar—just like a dream."

Near the end of February 1941, Yosemite hosted the Sixth Pacific Coast Intercollegiate Ski Championships. Seventeen colleges and two hundred skiers competed. However, a severe snow storm arrived without letup shortly before the races started. The 1940-41 Winter Club year book covered the story.

"No one not present could possibly picture the conditions that faced the seventy-eight college skiers entered in the cross-country, the first event of the schedule. Blinded and bogged down by the driving snow, and lashed by the gale which accompanied it, they struggled as best they could to cover the four-and-one-half-mile course that started from the Ski House. Some got turned around and doubled back on their tracks; others broke skis and ski poles in the heavy snow; still others lost the course completely when snow filled in the tracks. It was a wonder that as many finished as did—thirty-three brave and hardy souls." The downhill and jumping events were canceled altogether.

Two weeks later when Badger Pass hosted the Third Far West Kandahar on March 14 and 15, the weather was beautiful and snow conditions perfect. As important an event on the competitive level as today's world cup, the races attracted an international field of competitors and some of the most legendary names in skiing. Sir Arnold Lunn of Murren, Switzerland, known as the "Father of Slalom Racing," helped set the slalom.

Once again, Badger Pass's signature run Rail Creek was the site of the marquee downhill event. Widened the summer before with rocks and brush removed, the run no longer required racers to hug one side of the course. They could really let their skis run while three pairs of gates checked high speeds and demanded a few dramatic turns.

"It was difficult even for the keenest-eyed observers to predict who had won the downhill until the figures were released—so close were the first half dozen or so racers," wrote chronicler Ben Tarnutzer. "Not unexpectedly, Martin Fopp, former winner of the famed Parsenn Derby race of Europe, turned in the fastest time....a new record." Yosemite's Leroy Rust, Bill Janss and John Blatt all finished in the top ten. Yvonne Blossom also set a record in winning the women's race.

Lunn surprised the field the next day by setting an open rhythmically-quick slalom course. Yosemite's Chris Schwarzenbach edged out Bill Klein of Sugar Bowl to capture the two-run event. Peter Picard entertained spectators in spectacular fashion by "completing a somersault in the middle of the Big Hill and landing on his skis, continuing merrily on his way down to the finish line," noted Tarnutzer. Kathleen Starratt of the Lake Tahoe Ski Club won the women's slalom. An estimated five hundred skiers crowded into the Ahwahnee dining room for the award ceremony and to watch Arnold Lunn present the trophies to the elated winners.

The 10th Mountain Division was formed in 1943 from the 85th, 86th and 87th Mountain Regiments, drawing together an elite group of champion skiers, mountain climbers and European mountaineers for intensive training atop the Colorado Rockies. Their spectacular night climb of Italy's Riva Ridge was an important Allied victory in the winter of 1944-45.

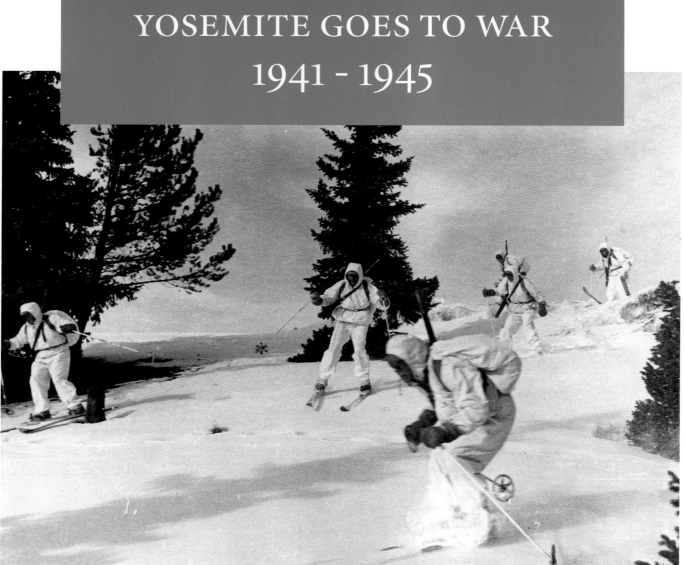

YOSEMITE GOES TO WAR
1941 - 1945

In 1941, a crisp autumn chill suggested an early ski season. Badger Pass opened Thanksgiving weekend, well in advance of its planned December 19th start. By early December reservations were already indicating full occupancy for the Christmas holidays.

On Sunday, December 7, late morning skiers were enjoying long swooping turns down the Big Hill. Pairs of skis stood upright in front of the porch of the Ski House as many ate their lunch in the warm sunshine. All were unaware of what was unfolding thousands of miles away in the Pacific.

Fresno ski shop owner Jim Huebner and his family were driving home at the end of the day trying to pick up a radio station in their 1939 Buick.

"Car radios weren't very good in those days and we couldn't get any station," recalls his son Larry. "We got all the way down the hill near Wawona when we finally picked up San Francisco. Then we heard the startling news. The Japanese had bombed Pearl Harbor! America was in World War II."

In the first winter season after the surprise attack on Pearl Harbor by Japan, Yosemite and other ski areas operated in an almost normal fashion, not yet touched by the war.

*Troops of the 10th Mountain Division
moving out over the snow.
In combat in northern Italy,
however, the weary soldiers would also
do a lot of slogging through the mud.*

Courtesy of the Far West SkiSports Museum

*Yosemite historian, Shirley Sargent, estimated that more than 150 residents eventually went off to war.
Badger Pass ski instructors Luggi Foeger, Arnold Fawcus, Jack Patterson and James McNamara
and others with ties to Yosemite such as David Brower and Bestor Robinson, would enlist
in the 10th Mountain Division to teach skiing and winter survival to mountain infantry .
Bill Janss had skied his way onto the 1940 Winter Olympic Team,
only to see his hopes dashed when the Games were canceled with the onset of war in Europe.
Bill, too, traded in his skies for a uniform.*

The first season after Pearl Harbor, winter sports at Yosemite went along comparatively untouched.
Yosemite's guest accommodations stayed open as did Badger Pass. Many of the men who enlisted in the service
were not called to active duty until after the ski area closed in the spring.
Gas rationing had not yet been implemented. Skiing and skating competitions went on as usual.
In January, the Ice Skating Carnival was held at the Curry Village rink,
and the Dodge Cup slaloms races were run at Badger Pass. The February schedule,
including the Washington Birthday holiday events, was held,
even though everything lacked the carefree atmosphere of the past.

On March 13 and 14, 1942, the Winter Club hosted the first National Championships held in California and the only one during the war. The races attracted fifty of the best skiers in the country including Alf Engen, Barney McLean, Sigi Engl, Gordy Wren and the University of Washington's Bill Redlin, the reigning 1941 national champion. Twenty women competitors included such stars as California state champion Catherine Henck and Gretchen Fraser, the women's national champion.

Charley Proctor, Yosemite's winter sports director, had supervised the immaculate grooming of the Rail Creek downhill and was predicting record smashing runs. However, it was not to be. A blinding Sierra storm swept into the park the morning of the race. It continued with renewed fury the next day during the slalom, accompanied by a high wind, so strong at times that it almost blew spectators off the slopes.

Nonetheless, the races continued. Sun Valley's squad dominated the women's races, taking seven of the top ten places in both the slalom and downhill, with Shirley

Skiing in a driving snow, Sun Valley's Alf Engen beat out individual winners Martin Fopp and Sigi Engl to capture the men's combined.

Racing for Sun Valley in the snow, Gretchen Fraser, who would win Olympic Gold in 1948, edged out teammate Clarita Heath by one-tenth of a second over two runs to capture the women's slalom.

McDonald outdistancing the field in the women's downhill and capturing the combined.

There was far more competition in the men's races. Martin Fopp of the Timberline Ski Club won the men's downhill. Amateur Barney McLean, racing for the Denver Ski Club, finished in a dead heat with the great Sigi Engl after the two runs of the men's slalom. The best that Yosemite could do that weekend were tenth place finishes by Lib Fitzgerald and Bill Janss in the women's and men's combined.

Sugar Bowl's Peter Picard crashed on the Rail Creek downhill. The recent European import passed too close to a tree and fell into its sun hole, injuring a knee. Peter recalled years later, "Alf Engen was behind me on the course. He could see that I was down and he told the race officials. Well, they hauled me down to the hospital in Yosemite Valley where Dr. Sturm put me in a full hip cast. The hospital gave me a bill for fifty bucks which was a lot of money in those days. I didn't have a dime, so they had to let me go. Well, about seven years later, after I got into dental practice, I finally had enough money to settle that debt."

Don Tresidder knew the war would not end quickly. He strongly believed that Yosemite could render a valuable service by raising the spirits of those working in the war effort. He knew that skiing and winter mountaineering would develop strong minds and bodies in the youth who would soon go off to war. He was determined to help with services and facilities.

"To all Yosemite Winter Club members wherever you may be, I send greetings and all good wishes. To all of you with whom I have shared the delights of Yosemite skiing, I send the assurance that the fires of friendship and warm hospitality will be kept alive throughout the period of our national emergency against the day when victory is ours and Yosemite's mountains again resound to the carefree cries of all of us who love and cherish the ski sport in the Yosemite tradition," Tresidder wrote in the 1941-42 Winter Club year book.

By the following winter of 1942-43, Yosemite had experienced drastic changes in its operation. Gas and food rationing severely cut park use and visitation. Tresidder had been forced to lay off half his

Don Tresidder poses on skis in the early war years.

In January 1943, Yosemite was soon to feel a great loss when Don Tresidder was named president of Stanford University. Tresidder had served on the university's board of directors since 1939, but the suddenness of his appointment caught an already war-torn community by surprise.

administrative staff. Many employees who hadn't enlisted or been drafted left for high-paying work in the defense industries. Rumors circulated that Badger Pass, and even the entire park, would be closed.

Food and fuel supplies were particularly limited. Families were given food stamps and rationing was often a hardship on those with children. It became a challenge for Charley Proctor to keep Badger Pass operating. "I spent two years with the phone to my ear, trying to get food for guests and employees in the Valley," Proctor remembered.

As winter approached, the park service committed to keeping the Badger Pass road open. The Glacier Point Mountain House and Ostrander Ski Hut would operate. Jules Fritsch had the rental skis in prime condition and Luggi Foeger, with all his instructors in the service and soon to go himself, stood ready to run a one-man ski school with volunteer help. With all the problems, Charley Proctor still had that pleased, far-away look in his eye which always came to him when he smelled snow on the horizon.

Sailors relaxing and at attention on the grounds of the Ahwahnee Hotel which served as the U.S. Naval Special Hospital.

"One day they borrowed some toboggans from good-natured Syd Ledson. They had no idea how to use a toboggan. A steep hill seemed to be a good idea—never mind a few large trees at the bottom. Anyway several of them got aboard and took off. They crashed into a five-foot-diameter fir tree. There were bodies smashed up with broken legs and broken backs. Some of the broken backs were so severe that they could never walk again," Charley Proctor recounted about the new naval residents in the park.

Tresidder's efforts kept Yosemite open, but visitation steadily dropped off. Attendance declined from 594,062 visitors in 1941 to 127,643 in 1943. In 1944, only 119,000 guests entered the park.

Hil Oehlmann, who like Tresidder had begun his career in Yosemite as a Camp Curry porter, struggled to follow the Tresidder legacy as general manager. It was a mixed blessing a few months later when the Ahwahnee Hotel was commissioned as a naval convalescent hospital. The hotel's elegant dining room became the mess hall; the Great Lounge was converted into a ward full of bunkbeds. Eldorado Diggings, the popular bar on the mezzanine, was turned into a Catholic chapel.

Yosemite offered a therapy of scenery and solitude for the sailors, far away from the horrors of war. Many of the military visitors were ambulatory. As Charlie Proctor recalled, "The men really wanted a city environment—bright lights and some shows to go to. I'm sure few of them appreciated nature, and they certainly didn't like the snow. Yet, the navy did provide recreation at Badger Pass for the men." After a few broken legs any sailor wanting to ski had to take a lesson first.

In the fall of 1943, superintendent Frank A. Kittridge announced that the ski area would be closed because of the lack of funds to keep the road plowed. Oehlmann argued that not only did Badger Pass help the sailors, but it benefitted the airmen from nearby Merced air base as well as civilians committed to the nation's defense. The park service found the funds to keep Badger Pass open.

Through the war winters, Badger Pass skiers now in the military occasionally appeared on the slopes during furloughs or while in transit. For many it was a special time, a melancholy moment, that held all the uncertainties of a nation at war. As a pilot for the air corps on transcontinental flights, Bill Cahow recalled how he often used Merced as an emergency landing site, rather than attempt the foggy airports in the Bay Area. "I got in a little skiing that way," he grinned.

Bill Cahow managed to get in some skiing during the war with his good friend Randy Rust.

California boys of the 10th Mountain Division relax in Glenwood Springs, Colorado. Donner Summit's Gratz Powers, Luggi Foeger and Lake Tahoe's Bill Bechdolt.

The war ended in August 1945. Unlike other notable areas such as Sun Valley and Sugar Bowl, Badger Pass miraculously had stayed open throughout the war. As a period of normalization began, employees and friends of the park anxiously awaited the return of loved ones.

Gail Rawles Brower, who taught school in Yosemite during the 1930s, recalls the delight and wonder of those years. "We didn't realize we were pioneering much of the ski action. We were having too much fun. It was the combination of social activities and competitive events that kept the Winter Club going.... Those were special times—unforgettable days."

WINTER CLUB FUN
1928 - 1942

S ince its formation in 1928, the Yosemite Winter Club's members continually
demonstrated a spirit and zest for life beyond the boundaries of winter
sports. Through their abiding reverence to the special world of Yosemite,
they created decades of magical, cultural experiences. At the same time,
they helped propel the once little-known fringe sport of skiing into one
of the world's most popular winter activities.

Against the backdrop of the waterfalls of the Valley frozen into columns
of diamonds against the towering rock walls, the Curry Company and
Winter Club launched an ambitious week-long program of activities
on December 22, 1928. Yosemite's winter wonderland was adorned in
Christmas finery. Holiday lights glittered from giant snow-clad trees.
Skating, skiing, sleigh rides and sliding down Ash Can Alley led the parade
of outdoor sports. There were baseball games on snowshoes, a costume
party and a skating gymkhana. Indoors there were dancing, dining and
motion pictures, almost everything anyone could wish for in the holiday
season. On two nights of the fairy-tale week, the Winter Club recreated
the summer firefall spectacle complete with plumes of flaming embers
cascading from Glacier Point into the dark abyss of the Valley.

*Shirley Ann Ewins from Los Angeles
learned to skate in Yosemite.*

The "Fancy Ice Skating Carnival" highlighted the organization's initial season. As one observer wrote that winter, "Brilliant illumination, soft-colored like jewels in snow embankments, silvery laughter of the merry skaters in their variegated and original costumes, skating to the rhythm of music—overhead stars—this was the skating ring, transformed for the evening into a veritable fairyland. A figure skating exhibition and the awarding of prizes for the 'Prettiest,' 'Funniest' and 'Most Original' costumes were a part of the program. Little Marion Albright (daughter of park superintendent Horace Albright), wearing her Dutch skates and a unique costume, which made one-half of her slim figure resemble a Dutch boy and the other half a Dutch girl, won the child's medal for the best costume."

In January 1931, the first San Joaquin Valley-Sierra Winter Sports Carnival was a huge success. The two-day event was sponsored by the California State Chamber of Commerce and the San Joaquin Tourist and Travel Association. Adding to the skating

Taking a break on the Curry Rink at the December 30, 1931, Winter Sports Carnival.

Costumes at the Fancy Ice Skating Carnival in 1929.

competition, snowshoe races and curling matches, there was even a "Tug of War on Ice for the Travel Information Girls," with San Francisco versus Los Angeles. The famed firefall illuminated the face of Glacier Point as a prelude to the crowning of Lois Laveen as queen of the carnival.

The selection of the queen of the winter carnivals was not based on looks, personality or vote gathering but rather on skill at skiing, ice-skating and snowshoeing. More than sixty years after winning the title and being crowned by California Governor James Rolph, Jr., in January 1934, Joyce Williams Boswell still remembers that exciting weekend. "They brought all nine of us up to the park and we stayed at the Ahwahnee. They had a one-day competition to determine the queen. I represented the Madera Chamber of Commerce and won the [frontward and backward] skating events—I learned to ice skate at Bass Lake. I had never skied much but I tied for fourth in the skiing. All together, I got the most points and became the queen of the carnival."

Governor James Rolph, Jr., arrived from Sacramento dressed as the "Lord High Chancellor" to crown Fay Hibbard of Fresno as queen of the January 1932 Winter Sports Carnival.

Queen Joyce Williams with Governor Rolph at the January 1934 carnival.

Winter Club records reveal little about how event organizers managed to inspire such bacchanalian levity during the prohibition period. Don Tresidder's mother-in-law, Jennie Curry, known lovingly to all as Mother Curry, was a staunch teetotaler. She espoused strict abstinence but many avoided her watchful eye. Accounts tell of "moonshiners" operating in Yosemite, selling "demon rum" to the needy. Many write-ups of the Winter Club parties note that "cider" was served, and former park employee Steve Tripp recollects that light alcoholic beverages were readily available at those early celebrations.

The success of these winter programs was due in large measure to Tresidder's ability to befriend and enlist prominent Californians in support of the Winter Club. During its first decade, the club was supported by a variety of influential outdoorsmen such as President Herbert Hoover, California Governor Clement C. Young, Representative Harry Englebright and other politicians. These notable early members in return garnered the attention of other eminent people such as *Los Angeles Times* publisher Harry Chandler, and financiers A.B.C. Dohrman and James Schwabacher, each of whom served at one time or another as vice president of the Winter Club.

The park service clearly supported the club's presence. National Park Service director Stephen T. Mather and his deputy, Horace Albright, representing the highest levels of the service, endorsed the activities. Yosemite's chief ranger Forest Townsley served on the club's executive committee.

In January 1933, the Winter Club held a "skiing contest" on Ski Hill.
Surviving the small slope in style, not time, was what mattered.
Ski school director Jules Fritsch braved the future of his career by serving
as the judge and jury for the participants who included
his immediate superiors, Don and Mary Tresidder.

Queen Violet von Glahm and King Steve Tripp in their royal sleigh.

More than sixty years later, "King Steve" Tripp of Bethesda, Maryland, still remembers the excitement of that bygone day. "It was quite a celebration. We had a lot of fun. I was only twenty-one at the time, a bachelor living in the Rangers Club, and working for the park service as an administrative assistant."

SNOW DAY

"Snow Day" typified the colorful Winter Club events. The popular festivity marked the arrival of the first major snow of the season. As the 1932-33 winter approached, the actual date was left to chance. Who else but a bunch of mountain adventurers would schedule a festival for the first day of bad weather!

Snow Day's king and queen were determined by the popular vote of year-round Yosemite residents. Voters were lobbied aggressively. The club reported that "a dance was given at the Ahwahnee on November 19th at which campaign managers were allowed to exploit the virtues of their respective candidates. Cider, gum, candy and cigars were passed out in quantity to assembled voters." Voting took place a few days later with the results entrusted in secrecy to the park superintendent.

Snow eventually began falling the afternoon of December 8. By the following morning, six inches had fallen, clothing the enchanted Valley in wintry finery. At first light, the organizing committee gathered to call all residents to Yosemite Village. Fire alarms sounded, trumpeting the official start of Snow Day. A proclamation was read declaring the day a Yosemite holiday. A royal decree commanded everyone to join in the celebration. Amid howls and cheers, the results of the balloting were announced. Park employees Stephen R. Tripp and Violet von Glahm were declared the first king and queen.

The parade began shortly, led by the park service's new snowplow, fire engines and park rangers on horseback. A bright red sleigh carried a beaming Queen Violet and King Steve. As the royal procession made its way around the upper end of the Valley, the two monarchs gleefully waved to those assembled along the way. With the coronation completed, the fun and games commenced. In the afternoon, an organized ski trip traveled to the upper end of the Valley. Tired trekkers returned to Yosemite Lodge for tea and refreshments. That evening, a dance was given in honor of Queen Violet and King Steve at the Ahwahnee. Festivities continued long into the night.

President Herbert Hoover, a graduate of Stanford University and a close friend of Tresidder, sponsored the Hoover Cup, a perpetual trophy that was first awarded to the winner of the Pacific Coast Intercollegiate Ice Hockey Games in 1930. Over time, other leaders in commerce added their sponsorships to the growing showcase of trophies and awards.

As far as Tresidder was concerned, there couldn't be too many winter events and social activities. He and the Winter Club transformed Yosemite into a wonderland each weekend during the season. Despite a decade of difficult economic times, club membership continued to grow.

"Interest in winter sports is growing apace in California. We are waking to the fact that the California Sierra Nevada compares favorably with the word's best-known winter sports centers," boasted the club in 1932. "Skis and skates are becoming as necessary to Californians as golf clubs and tennis rackets."

The Winter Club always showed a bit of self-effacing humor. For the 1933-34 winter, four different teams

Skiing at Badger Pass in 1934.

Young snowshoers, February 1927.

staged a successful membership drive, recruiting more than 500 new members. In celebration, "the winning team dined on the best the Ahwahnee kitchen could cook up—a sumptuous eight-course dinner topped by roasted turkey. The losing team from the National Park Service dined on canned hash and topped off with Jello."

Throughout the winter, the club provided the social fiber which held the Yosemite Valley community together. Early resident Everett Harwell explained that, during the busy summer tourist season, most permanent residents spent their time cleaning rooms, busing tables or building trails. There was little time for socializing or recreation. Winter provided the opportunity to step back and enjoy the park and their neighbors.

At the annual Christmas parties hosted by the Curry Company in the old Pavilion, "Uncle Don" Tresidder played a generous Santa Claus, bestowing skis, ice skates, a bicycle or some other major gift on every youngster in the Valley. After the parties, many families would venture over to the ice rink for additional fun.

Struggling new skiers needed help improving their skills. In February 1934 the club initiated proficiency tests at Badger Pass under the watchful eye of instructors Gordon Hooley and Ralph de Pfyffer. Nearly two dozen club members, including Tom Sovulewski and Snow King Steve Tripp, completed the examination of simple right and left christiania turns.

The following year's testing was more serious. Standards were being set by the Sierra Club and the Ski Mountaineers of Southern California. The third class test required an applicant to climb a ski slope, then descend under control making left and right telemark turns and finishing with a clean stop. Of fifteen skiers attempting what today sounds like a simple test, only three qualified: Mary Tresidder, Tom Sovulewski and Jack Patterson. The three would later be counted among the titans of Yosemite skiing.

It appears that no one attempted the more challenging second-class test. To pass, a skier was required to complete four consecutive christiania turns in soft snow on a slope of not less than twenty-five degrees, then repeat on hard pack snow. This was followed by four continuous pure stems turns and four continuous jump turns, all in soft snow on a twenty-degree or greater slope—not an easy task on the seven or eight-foot skis of the day.

"Basically, you had to win a major race to be considered for the first-class examination," one veteran explained. At the opposite end of the spectrum, the fourth-class test expected a skier to do a "one-and-two step stride; kick turns, both right and left; side step both uphill and downhill; climb uphill in a Herringbone; complete a snowplow turn; brake to a stop on an incline; traverse uphill and downhill; and make a 150-foot ski run," all without falling.

Bob Richmond, a skiing enthusiast from Fresno, first hit the slopes while in high school. Bob recalled, "In the mid 1930s, the road from Fresno to Wawona was still under construction in a couple of places. It was a long, tough trip to get up to Badger. At times we tied rope around the tires for chains to get there. We managed to miss the big storms, but going skiing was an adventure; it wasn't for sissies. I had a pair of eight-foot-long maple skis with a single leather toe strap. We would walk up the hill and put on the skis, one trip after another, trying to do the telemark turn—that was 'the thing' to do in those days. I eventually passed the third-class test. They were quite the deal."

When Charley Proctor became director of ski operations in 1938, he placed more emphasis on proficiency tests. He added a fifth-class test for entry-level skiers. And he replaced the dreaded telemark in the second class test with two sets of swing christianias. Few mourned its passing.

The Winter Club also introduced its own examinations and awards. The Gold and Silver Tests were timed runs against the clock and held on the main slope of Badger Pass. The more difficult "Y" tests went down Rail Creek. To qualify for the Gold, a racer skied from Ski Top down to the finish line in front of the lodge. The distance, nearly a mile in length, had to be completed in three minutes. As skiing technique improved, the times for these awards were reduced significantly.

Highly coveted pins were awarded for each test. In the space of two winters, early Winter Club member Roger Pirie managed to claim the Silver Ski, Gold Ski, Fourth Class, Third Class, Bronze and Silver Y. Fifty-five years later, while proudly displaying his various pins, he still recalls those eventful days. "The Y runs went down Rail Creek for 1.9 miles with a vertical drop of approximately 2,000 feet. To garner a Gold Y a woman had to complete the run in under five minutes and thirty seconds. Men skiers were required to ski it in three minutes or less. Silver Y and Bronze Y allowed longer times. Located on a south-west-facing slope, the exposure often afforded less than ideal snow conditions. The snows could be quite good on top, but would often be marginal below."

While skiing was quickly growing into the park's most popular winter attraction, ice-skating in Yosemite Valley was far from ignored. Throughout the 1930s, the Curry Village ice rink continued as a focus for club activities. Each season there were carnivals, local and collegiate hockey matches with a sprinkling of professional exhibitions, speed skating championships, and figure skating championships and exhibitions.

In late January 1935, a series of heavy snowstorms dropped several feet of snow. Keeping the rink clear was challenging work, but when the Third Annual Figure Skating Championships opened, Columbia Studio's newsreel cameras captured the pageantry on a smooth, glassy center stage.

"Every seat in the grandstand was taken and a large group of skaters watched the program from the rink," reported the club annual. "The snowbank surrounding the sides of the rink was ten feet high, . . . and brightly colored glasses with candles were set in the snowbank opposite the grandstand, forming a beautiful background for the skaters' bright costumes."

Skating at the Camp Curry ice rink under the spectacle of Half Dome.

The club really came into its own in the second half of the decade, with a steady stream of social and competitive activities. "Warm up for winter" conditioning and training classes were held in the park and sometimes in San Francisco and Los Angeles. While Badger Pass often had skiable snow by the end of November, the official opening of the season, snow or no snow, didn't usually happen until the second week of December. The ice-breaker was the "Club Frolic," an informal skating party at the Camp Curry ice rink.

Snowfall was the gift everybody wanted for the Christmas holidays. Club members looked forward to cheerful festivities which included the Yule Log, the arrival of Santa Claus and the Bracebridge dinner. So popular were these traditional events that, even in the Depression years of the 1930s, club members found themselves competing for room reservations.

In the new year there was no time for rest. A hectic schedule included weekly races and carnivals, and always the proficiency tests and the Sunday Slalom.

The Winter Club's first hockey team in 1928 (Wayne Morris, "Woof" Greeven, Curley, Art Morgan, Jim Connell, Gordon Hooley, Francis Fox).

Gordon Hooley, Gabe Goldsworthy, Emily Hoag and Earl Myr in February 1933.

Leroy "Rusty" Rust in 1933.

The Oakland American Legion plays the Winter Club team.

John Woods and Helen Thorns of Los Angeles,
California State Figure Skating Championships,
February 1933.

The Yosemite Ski Slide opened in December 1936
for two months on the Terrace Roof of
the Fairmont Hotel in San Francisco.
The eighty-foot long, thirty-percent slope
was covered with borax,
which gave much the same ride as snow
and, of course, was far more practical.

Hannes Schroll leads the troops in twice weekly conditioning classes in November 1937.

Each winter, success was measured by the number of events the club fit into the season. In the winter of 1939-40, the program included nearly thirty different activities, not counting the Friday night informal gatherings. "Every winter weekend or holiday, the Winter Club had something going," recalled Herb Blatt, a veteran member.

Socials included dancing, games and endless ski banter. By the late 1930s, even distant club members from the San Francisco Bay Area consistently arrived at the Ahwahnee on Friday night. "Tresidder had a small band that got the weekend going," recalled club veteran John "Boots" Blatt. "Some of those from the Bay Area might not arrive in the park until 11 p.m. but they would drop by the Ahwahnee to party before checking into their rooms. We would have a great time dancing, partying and talking skiing well into the night. Yet early the following morning, everyone managed to stagger out of bed and head for Badger."

After a full day of skiing, members looked forward to the Saturday evening party at the Ahwahnee.

Snowmen and friends in 1938.

Veteran ski instructor Bill Cahow recalled the warmth and camaraderie of those winter weekends and holidays. "Those gatherings were fabulous. There was a ten or twelve-piece band. Most of the time they were in the lounge. But on the big weekends they would move out into the Great Hall. And the food, it was equally fabulous. Tresidder brought in visiting chefs, and they each tried to outdo the other."

Within its first decade, Yosemite held more than one hundred major winter sporting events

under the leadership of the Winter Club. At its zenith, during the halcyon days before World War II, the schedule of activities staggered the mind and tested the muscles. The club emerged as a leading force in the evolution of American skiing, as sponsor of such major competitions as the Intercollegiate Races and the Far West Kandahar.

While competition was heated, fun was a primary goal. There was a spirit of fellowship and pioneering in the prewar years that reached beyond racing. The popular Inter-Club Races, started by publicist Ben Tarnutzer in the late 1930s, brought together three ski clubs for

Having fun on Ash Can Alley.

a spirited race. The San Francisco club's moniker was "Slide and Glide." The Southern Skis from Los Angeles were dubbed the "Porch Sitters" and Yosemite's team was appropriately named the "Tall Timber and Deep Canyon."

The Inter-Club competition included everything from serious to slapstick skiing. Sometimes, participants added rather dubious racing techniques to the course. The 1941 meet centered around a fun contest complete with racers in costumes. Others challenged themselves, and the laws of gravity, in trying to complete the course. "With a field of this caliber it is no wonder many spectators took their sleeping bags with them, even though the days were getting longer," reported the club's annual. "The contestants ranged in skill from bad to fair. However, the entrants all seem to be first-rate skiers, although according to the somewhat vague eligibility rules, no entrant may have ever competed in any but 'fun' races. Sometimes, a team is darkly suspected of slipping in 'ringers' but, so far, no proof has been unearthed."

Ben Tarnutzer and Miss Story take a spin in the Valley, February 1938.

Ben "Flash" Tarnutzer reported on the events in the 1941 Winter Club annual. "...The downhill went on schedule," he wrote, "which surprised no one other than the entrants. Heedless of life and limb, fired with a fervid desire to get the thing over as soon as possible, they turned their skis loose and tore down the slopes (and one or two evergreens that had the temerity to get in their way), barreled through the control gates in the saddle, flew down the lower part of the Big Hill and shot

between, under and over the finish flags in times that made the judges shake their stopwatches."

"And what happened to the [Winter Club's] Tall Timbers?" he asked. "Perhaps they got lost in their deep canyons." Adding to the fun, "Barbara 'Waikiki' Courtwright breezed down in (you guessed it) a grass skirt and lei," he remembered, "while Marshall 'Glamour Pants' Hall crossed the finish line in a top hat and tails, and carrying an umbrella, as thousands cheered."

Curling at the Camp Curry rink, February 1939.

For youngsters growing up amid the parade of winter activities, Yosemite seemed like a fantasy land. "On every weekend and holiday of the winter months, there was something going on. People wanted to come to Yosemite to skate or ski, or just to see what was happening. It created a fairyland atmosphere. There was no better place to grow up," recalled the late Leroy "Rusty" Rust.

The interruption of World War II forever changed the Winter Club. While the social activities resumed to some extent after 1945, the big carnivals and national ski races ended with the war. Instead emphasis shifted to the junior ski program, the North-South, Silver Ski and other interclub races, and new club activities in the backcountry.

For seventy years, a long line of Winter Club members chased the magic of winter sports. The beloved club, despite the challenges of winter, persevered. Today, the pioneer organization endures as one of the oldest and most respected winter sports clubs in the West. Its dedication and commitment to skiing is

"Now what do I do, dad?"

Daytime and moonlight sleigh rides were popular pastimes in the Valley.

evidenced by the numerous members inducted into the U.S. National Ski Hall of Fame. Included are Yosemite legends Hannes Schroll, Charley Proctor, Corty Hill, Al Sigal, Luggi Foeger, Sir Arnold Lunn, Byron Nishkian, Stan Mullin and Bill Janss. Two other Winter Club greats, Nic Fiore and Leroy Rust, have been nominated and, assuredly, their names soon will join the other Yosemite Winter Club alumni.

"Badger Pass is the best place to learn to ski and a wonderful place for family skiers,"
says ski school director Nic Fiore who taught an estimated 100,000 people how to ski.
"There are a lot of ski areas with bigger mountains and more lifts, but none of them have the family
atmosphere of Badger Pass. Yosemite is absolutely the best place in the world to learn to ski."

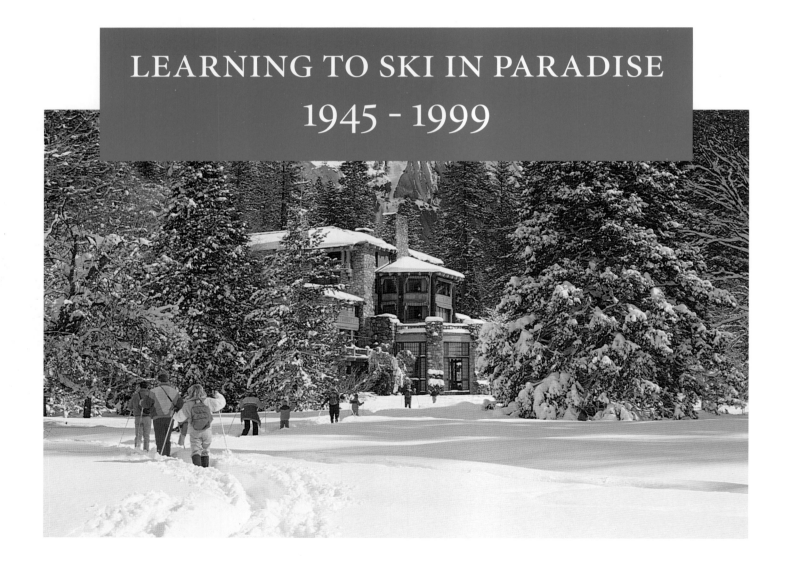

LEARNING TO SKI IN PARADISE
1945 - 1999

Badger Pass celebrated the end of World War II much like the rest of the country. Park employees and Winter Club members embraced the returning veterans. They grieved over their twenty fallen comrades who would never return home. Many others, wounded and invalid, only had their skiing memories.

With the coming of winter, skiers began drifting back to Yosemite and the serene slopes of Badger Pass. Gas and food rationing were over and a return to normalcy was slowly developing.

"We were all glad to get back to the slopes. Skiing had been such an important part of our lives, and many of us had gone through the war living for the day we could get back to Badger," remembers Bill Cahow, who flew transport planes ferrying troops and supplies around the country.

Yosemite ski instructor Lorin Trubschenck served as a B-25 bomber pilot in the Pacific and was awarded the prestigious Air Medal for heroic service. He was stationed in Japan on the island of Hokkaido briefly after the war. During the occupation he helped survey and develop plans for the Sapporo ski area, site of the 1972 Winter Olympic Games.

Lorin Trubschenck kicking up powder.

Other familiar faces reappeared on Badger's slopes. The Blatt brothers were once again blasting through the race courses. Olympians Bill Janss and Boots Blatt teamed up on the ski patrol. Bill was soon elected vice-president of the Winter Club. Popular skier and racer, Yasi Teramoto, was happy to be back. The proud San Joaquin Valley farmer of Nisei heritage was forced to spend much of the war in a California internment camp.

81

Second-generation Yosemite skiers were also coming onto the scene. Leroy and Jane Rust were on skis with their young son Randy. Michael Adams, son of photographer Ansel Adams, became a regular on the slopes. And Mary and Charley Proctor were there, of course, along with their three toddlers in hand-me-down skis and clothes.

Luggi Foeger was released from duty in December 1944 and arrived back in Yosemite in time for spring skiing. The Curry Company put him to work for the summer as assistant manager at Camp Curry.

Badger Pass looked vastly different to Luggi after his wartime experiences and months of separation. The beauty and natural wonders of Yosemite impressed him more than ever before. "So few have seen it when it glows with the richness of deep auburn, and the sparkle of late afternoon blueness," he wrote in an essay in *Western Skiing*.

However, before the next winter season was under way, the ever restless Foeger accepted a position at Grey Rocks Inn, a ski resort in the Laurentians outside of

Courtesy of Bill Cahow

Long time Yosemite skier Lorin Trubschenck, far right, took over as director of the Yosemite Ski School after Luggi Foeger left for Canada. The first post-war instructors were Leroy Brooks, Bob Lint, assistant director Bill Cahow, Mike Hughes and Arnold Burch.

The staff had grown by the next season. Pictured are Bob Lint, Bud Smith, Arnold Burch, Leroy Brooks, Don Rivers, director Lorin Trubschenck, Bob Brelsford, Marvin Olsen, Tony Freitas and Edvi Aro. Bill Cahow had taken the season off.

St. Jovite, Quebec. In an open letter to his friends and pupils in Yosemite, Foeger made clear his love for the West and the possibility of his return.

"We'll be thinking of you. All of you. For in our hearts, as perhaps in yours, is the undying hope that skiing in Western America will soar to unbelievable heights now that the war is over. The West has so many great opportunities for better and better skiing. Take advantage of them. Develop them carefully, and well."

Bill Cahow took over from Lorin Trubschenck as head of the ski school for the 1947-48 season. Before the war, Bill had worked for Luggi as an instructor.

"When I first started skiing, I would climb the hill at Badger because I couldn't afford a lift ticket for the Up-ski," he remembers. "I used to watch Luggi give instruction, and I picked up on his technique and learned to ski. Sometime later, he watched me come down the hill and came over and asked me if I would like to work for him. Of course I said 'yes.' That was a great deal because I got paid for it, and I got a lift ticket and a meal out of it."

Bill Janss was a top skier from Stanford before the Second World War.

Bill racing in the third Far West Kandahar in 1941.

Brother Ed Janss showing off in 1940.

BILL JANSS
FIRST YOSEMITE OLYMPIAN

Bill Janss began skiing at Yosemite in the early 1930s. He made the ski team at Stanford University for which Badger Pass was a regular training hill. Bill earned a place on the 1940 U.S. Olympic team, only to see the Winter Games canceled because of World War II.

In 1938, while skiing at Yosemite, Bill met Anne Searles, a pretty skier and his bride-to-be.

For their honeymoon in 1941, the newlyweds toured the other emerging ski areas of North America. On the brush slopes of Mont Tremblant they watched the young French Canadians coming down the hill on barrel staves. They discovered the terror of narrow New England ski trails and "boilerplate" snow. They took in the famous Dartmouth Winter Carnival, where they watched the home team vanquish the visitors from Chile. Then it was on to the National Downhill and Slalom Races in Aspen, where they saw their Yosemite ski buddy Boots Blatt finish sixth in a field of nearly seventy racers.

But for them Badger Pass was still the best. "What a pleasure it was to be on home slopes again with good spring snow, the best ski school in the country (we inspected quite a few) and running a race with people who could eat a hearty meal before the downhill and walk away whole after it," wrote Bill and Anne.

Eventually they moved away from the Sierra Nevada and became involved in property development at growing ski resorts such as Aspen. In 1964 Janss bought a floundering Sun Valley resort and launched a major refurbishment, putting millions of dollars into creating a year-round resort.

Anne Janss was killed in an avalanche in the Sun Valley backcountry in the early 1970s. In 1977 the Janss Corporation sold Sun Valley to R. Earl Holding. Bill remarried and remained committed to skiing until his death in 1996.

For more years than most of their competitors cared to remember, the three Blatt boys, Bob, John "Boots" and Herb, dominated California ski racing. In one 1946 race at Badger Pass, three out of the five top racers were Blatts, with Boots coming in first.

"You might beat one of them one weekend. But you always found yourself facing another one at the next race. And there were three of them. They were a force to be reckoned with," observed veteran racer Yasi Teramoto shortly before his death in the early 1990s.

The brothers were introduced to skiing in Seattle as youngsters. "My folks had skied in Europe and they wanted us to know the sport," remembers Boots.

In 1937, when Bob, the eldest, was a teenager, the family moved to Palo Alto, California. From there Yosemite was only a five or six-hour drive away, and for them Yosemite and Badger Pass were a skier's heaven.

On winter Fridays after school, the family jumped into their Packard and headed for Yosemite Valley.

After a full day of skiing at Badger on Saturday, the boys and their friends would gather in their Valley cabin to partake of Mrs. Blatt's Philadelphia pepper pot stew. It was a skier special, Yosemite-style.

On Sunday it was back to the slopes. Sibling rivalry pushed the trio ever faster. "We used to ski down Rail and Strawberry Creek" says Boots. "Those long runs were always challenging because they had such a major elevation drop, and you got into all types of snow."

He recalled that Patsy Janss, the sister of skiing great Bill Janss, used to be their "ski lift." By shuttling the boys back to Badger Pass in her car from the trail's end at the Wawona Road, she helped them get in at least two runs a day.

"Charley Proctor had us skiing under the banner of the Winter Club, going to distant ski competitions," recalled Boots. "The principal at Palo Alto High School knew we were good students so he allowed us to take off for two or three months for the racing circuit. We would take our books along and do our homework. In those days the host

club provided the room, board and lift ticket, so we didn't need much from the club.

The brothers went anywhere there was skiable snow. They were among the first North American competitors to ski in Chile. They raced the famed summer competition on Mount Lassen.

After military service in World War II, they stormed back to the slopes and the racing circuit—the Far West Kandahar, the Silver Belt at Sugar Bowl, the Harriman at Sun Valley, the Nationals at Mount

Hood, the FIS at Alta and other world-class events. Bob and Boots made the United States Ski Team for the 1948 Winter Olympics in St. Moritz, Switzerland.

Bob placed fifth place in the slalom. Unfortunately, Boots broke his ankle during training at Sun Valley, but still managed to make the trip.

"We were definitely ski pioneers … putting up with all the difficulties of skiing at that time. But those were the best of times," recalled Herb years later.

Boots, Bob and Herb, the notorious Blatt brothers, at the Old Jocks Race in the early 1990s, a few years before Bob's death.

Grudging approval by the park service for a Constam T-bar lift required that the towers be "folded down" when the snow was gone! Installed for the 1946-47 season, it was a giant step forward—still not a real lift, but infinitely better than the Up-ski that was soon destined for the scrap heap. Skiers loved the much faster tow which let them keep their skis on. However, there were more than a few problems. Bill Cahow recalled the inaugural day when he and ski instructor Tony Freitas were among the first T-bar victims. "It wasn't adjusted right, and instead of pulling us along as we rode on our skis, it lifted us off the snow and Tony fell off. I hung on and made it to the top."

Originally, the National Park Service had refused to sanction the installation of chairlifts at any of its ski areas. However, the resurgence of post-war skiing reinforced the call for additional uphill facilities at several national parks. This forced the service to reexamine the vexing issue of winter sports development. Both insiders and outsiders were concerned with the intrusion—particularly of downhill skiing—on the natural

The new Constam T-bar shares the hill with the Queen Mary Up-ski.

The wait for the T-bar looks long but skiers moved right along—at least until someone got tangled up.

integrity of the land. Some critics, even dedicated ski pioneers such as Dr. Harold Bradley, a frequent Yosemite skier and president of the Sierra Club, felt the proliferation of mechanical ski lifts, big ski races and winter carnivals were incompatible with the preservation of park land and the fundamental mission of the park service. Other voices objected to the removal of vegetation for ski runs and tows. Preservationists won many of the heated debates. Rope tows were removed at Mount Rainier and Crater Lake, ending downhill skiing at those western parks.

Arguments raged over the future of winter sports in Yosemite. Even though Badger Pass had ripened into one of the West's favorite winter playgrounds, park service bureaucrats believed that commercial skiing conflicted with park values.

In 1948, Bill Cahow attended a public hearing in Los Angeles on possible cutbacks of winter activities at Yosemite. "The company and the ski industry were very concerned with this proposal," remembers Bill. "Charley Proctor asked me to attend. He wanted a war veteran to testify. I agreed to do it, but I didn't know what to say. Proctor told me to say what I thought. I was very nervous, but I got up at the meeting and told them that I thought the idea of closing downhill skiing at Yosemite was really bad and that it should be allowed to continue."

Hil Oehlmann, Curry Company's general manager, pleaded its case, citing the service's long history of supporting and promoting winter use and recreation and stressing that winter sports were vital to successful year-round operations. The company had relied upon assurances that Yosemite was one of the parks where development for winter use was an established policy. "Without [Badger Pass] it would be ruinous for us to maintain our winter facilities in Yosemite Valley on any such scale as the present," he wrote in a letter to park superintendent Frank A. Kittridge.

The voice of reason prevailed and the proposal to close Badger Pass was quietly dropped. Nonetheless, park officials began taking a much closer look at subsequent company requests for new services and facilities. Large ski meets, such as

the intercollegiate races and the pre-war winter carnivals, were gradually scaled back. War surplus snow-tracked vehicles that brought visitors to Ostrander Ski Hut were allowed to continue, but only after much scrutiny.

In January 1948, the Yosemite and Stanford communities received sad news. While on a business trip to New York City, Don Tresidder had died of a heart attack at only fifty-three. Employees and friends of Yosemite grieved over the loss of a great man who brought winter sports and a new way of life to Yosemite.

After the 1947-48 season, Luggi Foeger returned to Yosemite from the cold of Canada to be reinstated as director of the ski school, letting Bill Cahow move on to a much needed career and something more than a seasonal job. Foeger brought three enthusiastic and athletic Canadian recruits with him—Ross Moore, Jim McConkey and Nic Fiore—to help teach students at Badger Pass.

That summer, Luggi put his Canadian contingent to work clearing the popular Rail Creek ski trail that had become overgrown

with brush during the war years. "We got permission from the park service and spent most of the summer clearing it out and widening the run in a few spots," recalled Nic Fiore. "It was tough work. We had to use hand tools— an old whip saw—no chain saws or anything like that. But when we were through, the park service came in and complimented us on what a good job we had done."

Sugar Bowl's Bill Klein remembers a different story. "Luggi wanted to widen the ski trail, clear trees out around Rail Creek but couldn't because of the park system," recalls Bill. "That year they had early snowfall. Luggi went and cut down all these trees then stood them up in the snow. In the spring, when the snow melted, they all fell over. Nobody knew anything about what had happened."

Nic Fiore arrived in 1948, planning to stay in Yosemite for just one year, but fifty years later he was still there.

BRYNHILD GRASMOEN
OLYMPIC STANDOUT

In the 1948 Winter Olympic Games at St. Moritz, Switzerland, Yosemite fielded three of the twenty-five competitors.

While Yosemite's Bob and Boots Blatt had dominated the ski slopes of California for the better part of two decades, it was Brynhild "Bee" Grasmoen, an attractive nineteen-year-old teenager from Merced, who showed the way.

The American skiers were not expected to do much against the hotshot Europeans. "Though the American girl skiers are easier on the eyes than most of the foreign competitors—Miss Grasmoen is pretty enough to rate a Hollywood starlet role—the blunt truth is that our feminine slalom and downhill entrants haven't much of a chance at St. Moritz," one American ski writer observed before the Games.

He was wrong. Bee's teammate Gretchen Fraser from Sun Valley won a gold medal in the special slalom, the first for an American skier. And the young Grasmoen finished strong in all four alpine events, placing eleventh in the slalom, ninth in special slalom, twelfth in the downhill and fifteenth in the combined.

Bee had discovered the slopes of Badger Pass when she was a pig-tailed lass of nine. At first, she wanted to be an ice skater, not a skier. Her girlhood dream was to follow in the footsteps of Sonja Henie, the world famous Olympic skating champion of the 1930s.

Bee's father bought a pair of skis to surprise his daughter who reluctantly put them on one day at Badger Pass. She soon forgot all about ice-skating—skiing was the only way to go.

By age twelve she had won the California State Junior Championships. Although World War II and gas rationing limited ski activity, Bee found plenty of challenges. In fact, as a young teenager she helped change the rules so she could compete in races as an adult.

Bee went on to win the prestigious Silver Belt Race at Sugar Bowl in the spring of 1948. Her skiing career was cut short when she suffered serious injuries in an auto accident two years later.

Courtesy of Bernice Shields

Bee Grasmoen began skiing as a nine-year-old.

Racing the slalom at Badger Pass in 1941.

AL SIGAL - "MR. WINTER CLUB"

Al "Mr. Winter Club" Sigal's devotion to Yosemite spanned almost five decades.

He and his family discovered Badger Pass in the 1930s, and almost every winter weekend found them on the slopes. They quickly got to know the "Badger Pass family"—the Tresidders, Proctors, Foegers and members of the Yosemite Winter Club and other skiers. Soon they, too, joined the Winter Club. The Sigal family was among the first to make an outing to the Ostrander Ski Hut. Al's two sons, Al, Jr. "Tito" and Bill, joined the junior race program and became junior state champions.

Al joined the National Ski Patrol and the Far West Ski Association. In 1939 he was elected president of the Yosemite Winter Club, a post he held into the 1950s, longer than any other president. A veteran of the First World War, Sigal helped organized the ski patrol to search for military aircraft downed in the mountains during World War II.

He once joked that he had spent more time as a ski racing official than he had as a skier. He was manager of the 1948 United States Ski Team. He served as director of the organizing committee of the 1960 Games at Squaw Valley. Sigal's lengthy contribution to skiing was recognized with his election to the U.S. National Ski Hall of Fame in 1971.

Even after Sigal could no longer join his sons on the slopes, this passionate skier would spend winter days on the porch at Badger Pass, watching others do what he had come to love. For Sigal, who died in 1980, skiing was more than a sport. It was a way of living life to the fullest.

Al Sigal, with his wife Marguerite, receiving the U.S. National Ski Hall of Fame plaque from Byron Nishkian.

Skiing surged in popularity with the resumption of the 1948 Winter Olympic Games in St. Moritz, Switzerland. Yosemite's Bob and Boots Blatt competed for the American men and the pretty and talented Brynhild Grasmoen skied strongly for the American women. Al Sigal, president of both the Winter Club and the California Ski Association, served as alpine ski team manager.

Overall, the Americans didn't fare very well against the superior talents of the Europeans. Al Sigal recognized a need for junior racing programs in the United States. A resident of Atherton, California, and an executive with the Safeway supermarket chain, Sigal elicited the help of Leroy Rust to organize a strong junior race program in Yosemite. Rust would carry the torch of junior racing for the next forty years as coach of Yosemite's junior racing program.

Many park service employee children participated and it garnered support from the local school. Rusty and Charley Proctor ran "ski days" for local kids in the fourth grade and above. At noon every Wednesday, students took bag lunches and were bused to Badger Pass. Once at the ski area they were issued ski equipment and put into classes to receive what one youngster described as "the right kind of higher education: skiing."

Peggy Proctor Dean recalled the fun and excitement the midweek outing provided. "The Wednesday afternoon ski program was a favorite activity. The bus ride to and from Badger Pass was just as much fun as the skiing."

The best school program skiers moved gradually onto the Yosemite Junior Race Team, known as "Rusty's Crappie Kids." The team's roster included a long list of recognizable names out of the Yosemite phone book. For example, the 1953 team included Mary Lou Sturm (Gardner), Chris Foeger, Tim Berrey, Randy Rust, Peggy Proctor (Dean), Stuart During, Richie Quimet and Toni Culver.

There were few young ladies on the team, but the ones who persevered were a talented group. Toni Culver and Jeannie Evans (Lodwick) qualified for the Junior Nationals. Overall, Yosemite's junior race program provided fun and competition for many youths. Randy Rust, who eventually took over coaching duties from his father, estimates that more than three hundred youngsters participated in the original program.

The Junior Race Team, "Rusty's Crappie Kids."

Born in Lewis Memorial Hospital in Yosemite in 1946, Jeannie Evans Lodwick was the daughter of park ranger Marshall "Buck" Evans, one of Yosemite's pioneer winter rangers.

As a young toddler, Jeannie had a territorial advantage when it came to skiing. For several years, her parents occupied the ranger stations at either Chinquapin or Badger Pass.

"I must have been born with skis on because I can never remember taking lessons, yet I was always skiing. I usually rode up the old T-Bar between the legs of one of Luggi Foeger's instructors or one of the ski patrolmen," she recalled. "When we lived at Badger, all I had to do to go skiing was walk across the road."

Joining her Yosemite Elementary School classmates at the Wednesday afternoon ski school, Jeannie soon attracted the attention of Leroy Rust, coach of the Yosemite Junior Racing Ski Team. She became one of "Rusty's Crappie Kids." The race team was anything but easy. "For as long as

I can remember, I was the only girl on the ten-man team," she said. She raced at China Peak, Dodge Ridge, Mammoth Mountain and other ski areas and reached the top of the junior circuit in the Far West Ski Association.

In the competition in the 1960 Silver Ski Race, the young teenager beat out more than one hundred other women skiers. The same year she skied her way to the Junior Nationals at Sugarbush, Maine. Although she did poorly on New England "boilerplate," she remained a credit to Yosemite.

A few years later, her family moved to Crater Lake National Park. At Oregon State University, Evans became the first woman to receive a letter in skiing.

After graduation she moved on to Steamboat, Colorado, where she met the skier who would become her husband. Their four sons have become a new generation of competitive skiers, although far removed from Badger Pass. Three of them have gone on to become Olympic skiers, including Todd Lodwick, who ranked third in the

world in nordic skiing in 1998. Their skiing heritage, Jeannie says proudly, is part of a legacy that goes back to Badger Pass, her father Buck Evans and Leroy "Rusty" Rust, her venerated coach.

Today, still skiing, she looks back on her Yosemite winters with fond

Jeannie dwarfed by walls of snow on her doorstep at the Chinquapin Ranger Station during the record winter of 1951-52.

memories. "Rusty made me do what I didn't like to do, but then I ended up having fun at it. I was the only girl on that team and he took good care of me," she said. "They were great times."

"Rusty's Crappie Kids" in 1961: Ricky Sharp, Todd Sharp, Leslie Rust, Kathy McLaren, Danny Armstrong, Jeff Sharp, Randy Armstrong, Jeannie Evans, Frank Carter, Randy Rust and coach Rusty.

Leroy "Rusty" Rust called himself a "middle class millionaire," working and playing in one of the most beautiful places in the world. Born in Yosemite Valley in an early residential area known as Soapsuds Row, he had Yosemite in his blood.

He would often reminisce about those early days of skating on Mirror Lake, sliding down Ash Can Alley and slipping down the slopes of the old moraine in Yosemite Valley long before there was Badger Pass. And then there were the wonderful days of the winter carnivals when he won the skating events.

It was Rusty's love of skiing and winter sports that defined his life and made him one of Yosemite's foremost defenders. He had a way of smoothing out differences within the Yosemite community and getting people to work together.

Until his death in 1992, Rusty served as the Yosemite postmaster, acquiring the moniker "Mr. 95389," the park zip code. For many, he was the "mayor of Yosemite." In his

seventy-plus years in the park, Rusty had seen a dozen park superintendents come and go. He was never reticent about telling them how to run the park, because, as he pointed out, "they were only passing through."

More than anything, he was a skier's skier and a ski coach. For more years than most people can recall, he was the coach of the Yosemite Ski Team, which he lovingly referred to as those "crappie little kids."

He organized the Ancient Jocks Race as a way of getting senior skiers reconnected with their sport and with other Badger Pass skiers. It was a fun race. The only thing taken seriously was the participation. Rusty had to work at it, but he made sure that he always finished last.

In 1976 he and park ranger Pete Thompson made the first known ski descent of the infamous Ledge Trail from Glacier Point to Camp Curry. When word filtered out that

Coach Rusty with three of his charges.

he had participated in this admittedly risky exercise, Rusty sheepishly admitted that the downhill skiing was the easy part. The hard part was facing his wife Jane with the truth about the precipitous run.

Years ago, when asked about his inability to leave Yosemite, Rusty responded, "Why? The best is right here. Besides, I'd get lost if I couldn't see Half Dome."

Despite his territorial bias, Rusty skied throughout the Sierra, leading his young racers down the mountainside. In 1987 his many friends pooled their resources to send Rusty and his son Randy on a helicopter ski trip to the Canadian Rockies. That experience was "out-of-this-world skiing," he recalled later. "It was mind-boggling and beyond anything I had known."

He always maintained that "the Good Lord did not subtract from man's total time for those days spent on the ski slopes. We may not have the biggest hills, but we've got the greatest skiers."

More than just skiers, Yosemite National Park also attracted film companies such as Fox Movietone News. In the late 1940s, journalist, international adventurer and radio personality Lowell Thomas, Jr., visited the park. An avid skier, Thomas hit the slopes at Badger Pass during the day and returned to the Ahwahnee for his nightly broadcast.

But by the end of the decade, larger and more glamorous ski centers such as Sun Valley, Aspen and Sugar Bowl were luring a greater number of skiers. Nearby, China Peak and Dodge Ridge were offering central California skiers a tempting variety of runs, lift access and vertical drop. It was time for a real marketing push if Badger Pass was to survive.

Henry Berrey, advertising executive for *Westways* magazine, arrived in Yosemite in 1949 as public relations director to meet this challenge. An Army veteran, Berrey did battle for the park by championing Yosemite on radio stations, and in national and regional newspapers, and by hosting travel agents and ski media.

Selling the attractions of winter sports in Yosemite came readily to Henry Berrey, shown here on the far right with Fresno Bee *sports editor Omer Crane (far left), the paper's public relations director Don Trabing and Yosemite ski school director Nic Fiore. With their children involved in junior racing, Berrey and his wife Eileen were big fans of skiing. He became secretary of the Winter Club, although apparently, his skiing left much to be desired. The club annual lovingly described him as an "enthusiastic but uncontrolled" skier.*

With sales manager George Oliver, Berrey introduced the "Mid-Week Ski Special," one of the industry's first all-inclusive travel packages. For just $25 a day, a guest received lodging, meals, ski rental, lift ticket, lesson and transportation to and from Badger Pass. The packages were a roaring success. "You couldn't afford to stay home," one company official noted.

In the 1950s, a revolutionary metal ski design helped propel skiing's popularity. The Badger Pass Ski Shop was besieged with skiers demanding to buy Howard Head's new quick-turning skis. "We couldn't keep them in stock," remembers Nic Fiore. "They were sold as fast as we could get them in. Those first Head skis were chrome—natural aluminum—which caused the sun to reflect off their bare metal. Later on, they made them black to get around the reflection problem. They changed the course of skiing around the world."

The metal ski coincided with the introduction of stretch ski pants and modern form-fitting parkas. Suddenly, skiing became high fashion. Baggy ski pants vanished from the slopes overnight.

"The wait for the lift wasn't too bad if you could gaze upon a young gal in a pair of stretch pants," observed Badger Pass skier Roger Pirie. "They say that the two most important three-letter words in the skier's vocabulary are 'sex and ski' and stretch ski pants covered both."

In 1951, the Stanford Ski Club and the Yosemite Winter Club honored Don Tresidder by establishing the perpetual Tresidder Memorial Cup. Held at Badger Pass, the inaugural race resembled the pre-war meets when a dozen colleges and two hundred skiers were on the slopes. At the first race, nine colleges and about thirty-two competitors participated. Within a year, the four-way challenge that included ski jumping, cross-country, downhill and slalom skiing had become one of Yosemite's most popular events, continuing through the 1950s. An appreciative Mary Tresidder presented trophies to the collegians at a ceremony in the Ahwahnee Hotel.

Mary Curry Tresidder and her friend Lucy Butler on "snow bikes."

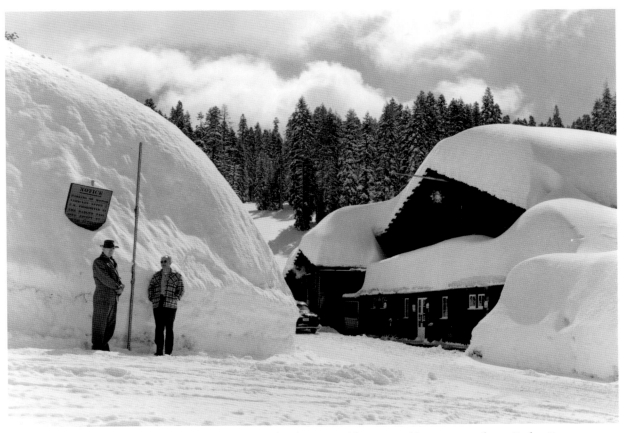

The winter of 1951-52 was the biggest on record to that time with snow reaching seventeen feet at Badger Pass. The same year Southern Pacific Railroad's City of San Francisco was stranded in the Sierra Nevada for six days.

With reluctant support from the National Park Service, the first North-South Ski Races were staged at Badger Pass in 1956. The competition was the brainchild of *San Francisco Examiner* ski writer Carson White. The event pitted the best racers from Northern California against their counterparts from the south.

"I was concerned that there were several Class C races but not many Class A races, so I promoted the idea of a Class A race," remembers White. "We tried to get ten men and five women on each team, but sometimes we came up short. I picked the northern team. We still had a lot of great skiers such as Tommy Corcoran, Boots Blatt, Georgine Bihlman, Pat Nast, Jimmy Nunn and others involved." Initially, racers competed in both downhill and slalom. After a few years the downhill on the uncertain snow of the Rail Creek course was discontinued in favor of three runs of the slalom.

Billed as "civil war on the slopes," the dividing "Mason-Dixon line" tended to move geographically from one year to another. Racers from Yosemite, such as Randy Rust, filled in where needed. Some skiers switched loyalties and showed up on the other side. Former Olympian Tom Corcoran captained the North Team until he moved to Southern California when he joined the South.

"It was serious racing because it involved a team effort," recalled Denver University's Jimmy Nunn who competed for the South. "The race got very competitive at times. Most other races were based on individual results but for this one we skied as a team. There were a lot of good racers out there pulling together."

The North-South Ski Race continued for a decade. The North captured six titles to the South's four. After ten seasons the event lost its financial support and was discontinued. "The *Examiner* had provided a nice trophy at the beginning, but I was paying for the other costs out of my own pocket and it just got too much," confessed Carson White.

Courtesy of Carson White

Carson White racing for the North.

Courtesy of Jimmy Nunn

Jimmy Nunn represented the South.

Bob Bergstrom, Charley Proctor and Carson White.

Pat Nast, Byron Nishkian and Trygve Berg,
with Herb Blatt in the background.

THE NORTH SOUTH RACES

Georgine Bihlman and Louis Fellows

The South Team in 1964.

The North Team about 1964.

Another important competition, the *Fresno Bee* Silver Ski Race, was introduced in January 1957 and continues to be a Yosemite favorite, attracting hundreds of competitors. Twelve separate classifications were devised based on age, ability and gender. Names of the overall fastest male and female were engraved on a four-foot-long Silver Ski, still prominently displayed in the Badger Pass Ski House. Yosemite junior racers dominated, such as Peggy Proctor, Jeannie Evans, Randy Rust, Rob Woessner, Lanette and Lynne Cross, and Lucy Furr Parker, with each awarded a silver pin that they proudly wore to school. During the 1960s, Yosemite's Frank Carter won his class five times. And in 1987, Leroy Rust's granddaughter Jessica captured first place.

Badger Pass hosted few other major events. The Far West Kandahar, the Nationals and the Pacific Coast Intercollegiate Ski Championships remained only in memory. The once unrivaled winter carnivals and skating competitions disappeared. Recreational ice-skating was still popular in Yosemite, but warm winter weather often turned the Camp Curry rink into a wading pond, forcing cancellation of events. The park service continued to be the bane of winter activity, discouraging large events and their crowds of spectators. Its philosophy was that recreational use of the park should be an individual, personal experience surrounded by the natural beauty of the park. The park service regularly denied permission for most events at the Curry rink and Badger Pass, even those not billed as "spectator events."

Tito Sigal created this cartoon in the early 1940s.

Parents and kids out on the slopes in this 1953 photo.

The Winter Club kept alive some of the carnival atmosphere of the pre-war years even if there were few big social events. During Easter break, the club ran costume and rope races, and an egg hunt on skis. "Have you ever skied tied to a partner by a rope; have you ever been in a slalom without poles, stopping at every other set of flags to pick up an Easter egg; or have you ever worn a costume while skiing? Believe it or not, all this and more happened at Badger Pass over the Easter holidays," promoted the club newsletter.

But the club was not quite as egalitarian in that period as it might have appeared. When young Dr. Charles Woessner arrived in the park in the early 1950s, he and his wife soon discovered that the Winter Club was not open to all. Al Sigal was then president and Bill Janss vice president. But the rest of the club officers including winter sports director Charley Proctor and secretary Henry Berrey were Curry Company employees. "It was something of a closed club, and still the publicity arm of the company," said Woessner. "It had the Stanford 'hangers-on' and the

'Curry Company faithful,' those who used the High Sierra Camps in the summer and skied at Badger Pass in the winter, and five of the seven club officials were company people. Through the years, the presidency rotated between Stuart Cross and John Curry. Henry Berrey was always the secretary. Occasionally we would get invited to a cocktail party. The Indian Room dinner dance at the Ahwahnee was open to any local, but it wasn't until the early 1960s that the club really opened up to the public."

Barbara Ann Ging shows off her figure skating at the Curry rink. Refrigeration equipment was installed in the summer of 1969, permitting year-round operation.

Weasel-joring, like skijoring behind a horse, was fun but dangerous. It was banned in 1976.

Don Tresidder's thirty-year-old dream of California hosting the Winter Olympic Games became a reality in 1960 when close to one thousand athletes from thirty-four countries gathered at Squaw Valley for the VIII Winter Olympic Games. Noted for their simplicity and feeling of community, they were celebrated as a huge success. The first-ever televised events attracted an estimated 240,000 spectators and shared the beauty of the Sierra Nevada with millions of viewers worldwide.

Although no Badger Pass skier made the United States team, Yosemite was well-represented during the Games. Al Sigal sat on the Olympics' Organizing Committee Board of Directors. Charley Proctor was a consultant for the alpine events. Henry Berrey, Leroy Rust and Byron Nishkian lent their time and talents to the games, as did members of the Yosemite ski patrol.

The success of the Squaw Valley Olympics produced a surge of development in the Tahoe Basin and throughout the western ski industry. Badger Pass, too, enjoyed a skiing renaissance. By 1962, visitation had increased enough to force the ski school to expand its staff to thirty instructors. In 1965, the park service finally allowed chairlifts to replace the antiquated T-bars. The parking lot was expanded to accommodate more cars and the renamed Snow Flake Day Lodge underwent needed renovations.

"Badger Pass was a busy place in those days," recalls Dave Downing who coordinated Winter Club special events for twenty years.

"Even though the big spectator events were gone, we were able to have all kinds of club activities and I tried to get people involved. There were races down Rail Creek, the interclub meets and Sunday Slaloms. Men and women alike would practice and practice, trying to trim a few seconds off their times. When snow was light, we would even go out into the trees and haul in snow on a toboggan so they could race."

The Flying Fifty race was especially popular. Started before the war, this permanent ladder recorded the names of the fastest twenty-five men and women who ran the Gold Ski course on the Big Hill. The list changed as the times got better over the years. The competition was discontinued in 1972 when the high-speed racing became too dangerous.

Junior racer Randy Armstrong in the early 1960s.

Nic Fiore took over the Yosemite Ski School when Luggi Foeger departed for Sugar Bowl in 1958. Much of Badger Pass's continued success stemmed directly from the athletic French Canadian. One of twelve children raised by Swiss-Italian parents, Nic Fiore was born in 1920 in Montreal. By the age of eight he learned to carve turns on the tame slopes of Mount Royal in the heart of the city. In 1946, he was certified as a Canadian ski instructor and taught in the winter and worked as sports director in the summer at the St. Adele Lodge in the Laurentians.

While at St. Adele, the amiable Fiore met Luggi Foeger when the legendary ski instructor was teaching at nearby Grey Rocks. Luggi, always on the lookout for new talent, convinced Nic to return with him to Yosemite in 1948. Nic came west with the intention of teaching one winter and then returning to Canada. When the year was over he packed up to head home. He never made it to the train station. "I just wanted to see California, to see what was here," reflects Fiore, who became an American citizen in 1955. "I somehow lost track of time." One winter led to another.

Nic Fiore with a young student.

It was snowing the night that Nic first arrived in Yosemite Valley and he couldn't see anything. The next morning, the storm had cleared. When he walked outside with Luggi Foeger, he saw the snow-covered cliffs and exclaimed, "But Luggi, where do the beginners ski?"

Fifty-two seasons later Nic still teaches students on the slopes of Badger Pass.

When Nic first arrived, the Badger Pass lodge was a solitary structure. There were rope tows and a T-bar—the Up-ski was gone and it would be almost twenty years before the first chairlift would be built. Employees boot-packed the runs. Though facilities were rudimentary, Nic immediately fell in love with the place. Gregarious, good natured and energetic, he quickly became a favorite of Winter Club members. "Nic added a lift to Winter Club dances. He would sing a songfest of ski tunes that would make you think you were in Chamonix!" said Mary Tresidder.

Nic's favorite fan was a young college student nicknamed Midge who worked during summer months at the Camp Curry dining room.

"A group of us would always go to the beach together," says Midge who married Nic in the early 1950s. "Nic spoke little English having grown up in French Canada, something I found a bit amusing seeing that his summer job then was at the Curry Transportation

Office where he had to direct people where to go. No one could understand him, but Nic was very outgoing. He was just a lot of fun to be around."

Yosemite's back country beckoned Nic, too. When winter wound down and the snow faded away, he traded his wool ski cap for a sun visor and moved to the equally challenging task of running the Curry Company's network of High Sierra camps. An accomplished athlete, he could easily outpace those on horseback heading to the camps, sometimes trekking over twenty miles in a day. Other times he ran between the camps, visiting two before supper.

"Nic never did like horses. He'd always send back any given to him. It was just us ordinary people who rode," says Peggy Proctor Dean.

Skiing was number one in his life, but Nic also loved biking. As a youth he raced on indoor oval tracks, pedaling a bicycle with one fixed gear and no brakes. A German pro team once presented him with a Durkopp racing track bike which he brought with him to Yosemite. One day during his first summer, Fiore sped down from

Nic Fiore with Peter Picard and Wolfgang Lert at the 1999 International Skiing History Association meeting at Mont Tremblant.

The Yosemite Ski School staff in 1980.

Badger Pass and through Wawona Tunnel going close to fifty miles an hour.

"There was a ranger and he starts blowing his siren at me," Fiore recalls. "I finally stopped ten miles further down. I didn't know the siren was for me. The ranger asked why I didn't stop. Didn't I have any brakes? In my broken English I told him no. The *look* on his face. He thought I was crazy."

"From the minute I became certified as an American instructor in March 1949, I became an officer of the Professional Ski Instructors of America," Nic says. "I've been treasurer, clinician and examiner, and was one of its first directors." In 1967, Nic attended the French National Ski Instructors School at the request of the French government. The following year he was an official delegate to the International Ski Instructors Congress in Aspen, Colorado.

"I ran the course with Stein Eriksen," Fiore recalls. "One day during some free skiing I was following Stein. He hit a bump and leaped seventy-five feet. I wanted to take my skis off."

When Nic took over the Yosemite Ski School in 1958, an all-day ticket at Badger Pass sold for $3.75. A single ride on the rope tow was just 15 cents. But crowds continued to dwindle as skiers headed to the more glamorous ski resorts. It didn't matter to the optimistic Fiore. If skiers wouldn't come to him, he would go to them. He initiated a program to promote skiing in the Fresno area. During the week, Nic traveled to city parks to conduct dryland classes. "I can recall some of those at Holmes Playground in Fresno where we had more than one thousand people out there on skis. I was up on a platform with loudspeakers, giving some of the basic instruction. Of course, the final lesson was up at Badger Pass."

Nic introduced a new, simplified method of instruction. He modified Luggi Foeger's rotating Arlberg technique. He taught his students to initiate the turn from the feet, and cut down on the amount of wind-up and rotation.

"Basically, I tried to keep it simple. No student should be burdened with a lot of technical jargon. Let them enjoy themselves and ski," says Nic. "I had great results."

HERE
COME
THE
PUPS

In addition, Nic emphasized teaching kids as soon as they could stand on skis. Today, Badger Pass's "Pups Program" for preschool students is one of the country's oldest and most established of its kind.

Under Fiore, Yosemite's ski school sometimes taught 900 lessons a day. In 1989, it taught 14,000 lessons in the month of February, and 34,100 during the ski season.

Nic has received many awards over the years. In 1971, the Professional Ski Instructors of America voted him "Most Valuable Ski Instructor." In 1986, Nic received the prestigious Charley Proctor Award. This honor is given annually by the western region of the North American Ski Journalists Association to individuals who have made outstanding contributions to the sport of skiing. In 1987, Nic was nominated to the U. S. National Ski Hall of Fame. The same year, he received awards from the Northern California Ski Media Association, the Nevada Ski Media Association and the Southern California Association of Ski Writers.

Nic is the author of the best-selling book *So You Want to Ski* published in 1965, and for many years he wrote a column "Ski Tips by Nic Fiore" in the *Fresno Bee*.

As Nic scans the slopes today, looking for a familiar face, he sees newcomers who bear a strong resemblance to those he taught early on. Some of his Pup Ski Schoolers are third generation Badger Pass skiers, perhaps the grandchildren of those he taught so many seasons ago. The club's longstanding proficiency tests and countless races have gone wherever old ski races go. Today's skiers and boarders speak a different language. The Geländesprung has disappeared, as have the reverse shoulder, the Ruade, Christianias and a host of other skiing techniques of yesterday.

Many of Nic's coworkers have fanned out across the country. Though the years, Badger Pass served as a prime training ground for these men and women, strengthened by the Curry Company's emphasis on hotel and resort training. Bob Maynard at Aspen; Pat O'Donnell at Kirkwood, then to Keystone before replacing the retiring Maynard; John Crofut at Sierra Summit and then Hood Meadows ski area.

Nic Fiore posing for his fiftieth anniversary poster.

"Badger Pass is the best place to learn to ski and a wonderful place for family skiers," says Nic, who has taught an estimated 100,000 people how to ski. "There are a lot of ski areas with bigger mountains and more lifts, but none of them have the family atmosphere of Badger Pass. Yosemite is absolutely the best place in the world to learn to ski."

The Yosemite Winter Club successfully weathered many challenges throughout its history, yet nothing affected it as much as the purchase of the Yosemite Park & Curry Company by the Shasta Telecasting Corporation in 1968. The Curry Company had supported and subsidized the club—membership dues were little more than perfunctory. U.S. Natural Resources, operator of the concessions at Crater Lake in Oregon and Mount Rainier in Washington, soon took over from Shasta Telecasting and terminated many long-term employees, including the spirited Henry Berrey. Things improved when the Music Corporation of America took over the concession in 1973. They reinstated the Curry name and brought modern business management to Yosemite.

Two other events also marked the end of the era. In 1970, the much beloved Mary Curry Tresidder passed away, ending seventy years of Curry and Tresidder family influence in Yosemite. A year later, Mary and Charley Proctor retired to the warmer climes of Scotts Valley, California, concluding thirty-three years of dedicated service.

The Junior Race Team at Station KJEO in Fresno in the 1960s.

Under the guiding hand of Leroy Rust, the junior racing program continued unabated. Yosemite youth competed far and near, in such races as the American Legion Junior Slalom, the Lions Club Slalom, the Levi Junior Ski Rodeo, the Fresno Bee *Silver Ski Race, the club's own junior trophy race, and the club slalom championship. "It was just like the 1930s, only more fun," remarked Rusty before his death.*

Mary and Charley Proctor with Al Sigal in 1971 when he received his plaque for the United States National Ski Hall of Fame.

Just as it did in the 1970s, the deck still attracts crowds for lunch in the sun.

Two consecutive drought years in 1975-77 devastated winter sports throughout the Sierra Nevada. The lack of snow allowed for a renaissance of ice-skating. With memories of years gone by, Yosemite skaters returned to Mirror Lake. With Tioga Road accessible for much of the winter, Rusty led trips to the frozen, snowfree surfaces of Tenaya Lake and other lakes in the high country, once even managing to trek to 9,000-foot Lower Cathedral Lake. The junior racing team substituted a game of ice hockey on Siesta Lake near White Wolf for runs down the slopes. "It wasn't very good hockey, but we had a lot of fun," Rusty's wife Jane remembered.

The Winter Club found itself quite literally on the rocks and membership plummeted to a handful of survivors. When park ranger Ron Mackie came in as president in 1979, he had the difficult task of picking up the pieces. Ron described how things got turned around. "By the late 1970s, the club was almost bankrupt. The membership was down to about fifty people. A group of us went over to Rusty's

house to discuss the situation. We learned that he was paying the expenses for the junior racers out of his own pocket. We knew it couldn't go on, so we went to Ed Hardy, president of the Curry Company and asked what we could do. He came up with a plan to sell memberships in the club, throwing in two free lift tickets at Badger Pass and two skating lessons. He gave the club free use of the Camp Curry Banquet Room and a kickoff dinner. It was a heck of a deal for fifteen bucks. The membership grew to about 2,500. We soon had money in the bank and could again afford to send the kids to junior races at the various ski meets. Ed Hardy deserves the credit for saving the Winter Club."

The Yosemite Winter Club endures as one of the most established and prestigious ski clubs in the world. With a healthy membership and year-round schedule of activities, the club continues to provide countless families access to the beauty and wonders of Yosemite National Park. A passionate outdoor spirit remains alive, propagated by a triumphant list of past and present members. The club's influence helped establish

© Chris Falkenstein

*Snowboarding is as big at Badger Pass
as it is at other resorts.*

and popularize the sport of skiing in North America. Its history mirrors the magnificence of Yosemite itself. Its personality epitomizes the character of skiing as it has evolved.

Even after skiing the same slopes for half a century, Nic Fiore remains enthusiastic about Yosemite and Badger Pass, with the magic of the mountains and the true spirit of skiing. "This is absolutely the best place in the world to live," says Nic Fiore. "It is a pleasure to be here. Living in Yosemite has been a honeymoon. A deep strength emerges from being in the mountains. You're in sync with nature and that gives you an inner strength, the energy you need. It's very deep and honest."

During the early 1930s, exploration of the Yosemite backcountry continued unabated. In 1932, Jules Fritsch and Ralph de Pfyffer (pictured below) made extensive reconnaissances of the high country beyond Glacier Point looking for new ski terrain.

THE OTHER YOSEMITE
1928 - 1999

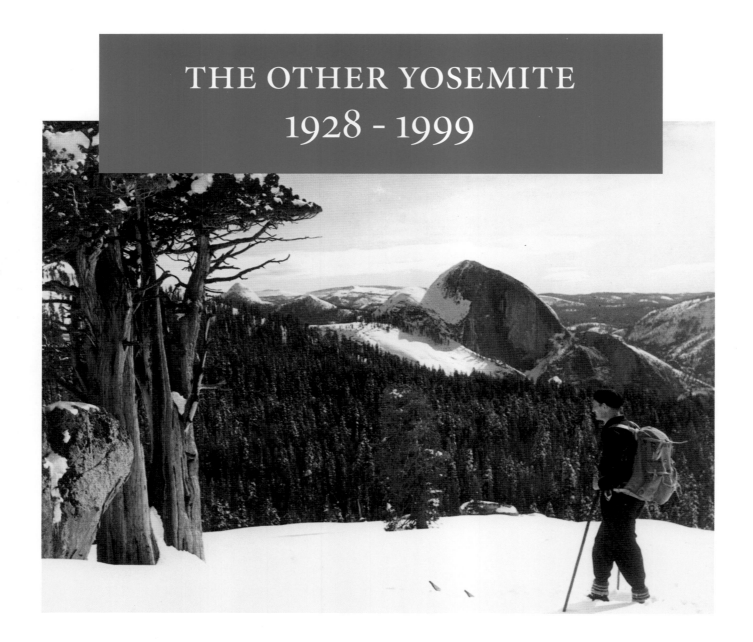

I n April 1929, a lone adventurer walked out of the Yosemite high country after completing one of the most daring and ambitious ski journeys of all time. Alone and unaided, Orland Bartholomew, a twenty-six-year-old stream gauger from nearby Big Creek, California, had spent the entire winter skiing along the crest of the Sierra from Mount Whitney, two hundred miles to the south.

During his epic trek, Bartholomew camped in the snow, sometimes under beautiful star-filled skies, other times hunkered down against a howling blizzard. Along the way he relied on food caches he had stashed the summer before. "Bart" made the first winter ascents of Mount Langely, Mount Tyndall and Mount Whitney, all exceeding 14,000 feet. As he threaded his way through snowbound passes and over roaring streams, he also made the first winter observations of the High Sierra, recording temperature, snow depths and wildlife sightings while taking notes and nearly four hundred photographs.

Sadly, the San Joaquin Tourist and Travel Association backed out of its promised support of Bartholomew's trip and thus the tale of his herculean exploits was not widely published. At that time, California's press and business leaders had little interest in any reports that the Golden State, the "Land of Sunshine and Honey," had snow and cold. During the 1930s, however, Don Tresidder and the Curry Company were able to turn this attitude around and tourist organizations became strong supporters of winter and its virtues. Snow and cold weather should be welcomed, not maligned.

"Bart" making camp near Mather Pass.

Orland Bartholomew.

When Tresidder first launched his winter programs in 1928, ice-skating, tobogganing and snow play were fine for most winter visitors to Yosemite. However, he also dreamed of opening up the vast reaches of the park's backcountry to ski touring. In January 1929, Ernst des Baillets led two of his staff and O. G. Taylor on one of the early explorations into the winter terrain that few had seen. They climbed the Four Mile Trail from the Valley on foot to the Mountain House at Glacier Point where they began to ski.

The Winter Club reported on this trip in its 1928-29 newsletter. "Mr. Taylor and his companions went on skis from Glacier following the road to Bridal Veil Creek until they were within half a mile of Badger Pass. On January tenth they spent the morning beyond Sentinel Dome. . . . They returned to the Valley about 4:30 p.m. via the Four Mile Trail." Five years later, after the opening of the Wawona tunnel, Badger Pass would become a permanent part of the winter scene.

Don Tresidder carrying skis and snowshoes on the Four Mile Trail to Glacier Point in 1928.

By the early 1930s, skis were stashed at the Glacier Point Hotel for those who trudged up the Four Mile Trail.

Snowshoers at Tuolumne Meadows ranger cabin in 1927.

The long runs on the slopes of Mount Watkins on the north rim of the Valley also beckoned the adventurous skier. A ski chalet here would give access to Mount Hoffman and the ranger cabins at Tenaya Lake and Tuolumne Meadows.

In the summer of 1929, Tresidder ordered construction of a cabin at Snow Creek, 3,000 feet above Mirror Lake. The cozy lodge, designed and built by E. T. Spencer of San Francisco, boasted a kitchen, common room and bunks for fifteen guests. In addition, the park service permitted winter use of the ranger cabins, and Tresidder equipped them as well for overnight guests. Cross-country skiers could now range all the way to Tioga Pass and beyond.

A six-day tour from the Snow Creek chalet, including a cook and guide, cost $65. A two-day tour ran $37—which included a packhorse to carry skis and supplies on the 2,700-foot climb from the Valley floor.

SNOW CREEK CABIN

Of the many artists and authors who have been moved by the magic of Yosemite, few have done more to convey that emotion than Ansel Adams, America's premier landscape photographer. His images have lured millions of visitors from around the world to the park. As much as Adams revered Yosemite, he also wanted it protected from too much attention.

Before his death in 1984, Ansel would reminisce about the winter trips he made into the Yosemite backcountry in the late 1920s and early 1930s. He helped harvest ice from frozen Merced Lake on the "icehouse runs." With his young bride Virginia Best Adams, he visited snowbound Glacier Point. On more than one occasion, he accompanied ski school director Jules Fritsch to the slopes above Tuolumne Meadows.

On one such trip in the winter of 1929-30, Fritsch and Adams set out from the new Snow Creek chalet with a group of Yosemite Valley friends. The week-long trip took them to Tenaya Lake and Tuolumne Meadows. "It was a great experience to see the Yosemite high country in winter, and I managed to learn a little skiing.... We had a good time," he recalled years later.

In the summer months, Adams climbed numerous tall peaks, making several first ascents along the southern boundary of Yosemite, including one 11,000-foot peak that now bears his name. Whatever he did, it was with enthusiasm and passion. He was a talented pianist and effective writer, and he had few equals as an ardent spokesman for preserving wilderness and the environment.

His eloquent 1932 article in the *Sierra Club Bulletin* is set against the stunning backdrop of a brilliant whitewashed mountain world, when he and the indomitable Fritsch clamored out of their snowbound cabin at Tuolumne Meadows.

"After several days we emerged on a new and glorious environment, for the storm has piled a great splendor on the world, and peak and forest gleam with frosty beauty. The morning is clear and cold, the last stars burn with diamond light as we cross the meadows on our long run to Merced Canyon.... At Tuolumne Pass we find true alpine conditions—supremely fine snow, swift and dry; grand open areas above the last timber, undulating for miles under cobalt skies; peak and crags flaunting long banners of wind-driven snow. A world of surpassing beauty, so perfect and intense that we cannot imagine the return of summer and the fading of crystalline splendor encompassing our gaze.

"The white magnificence yields to the clean motion of our skis, and we glide down over the glistening dome of the world and launch our descent to the Merced River. Down we rush cutting the sharp air with meteor motion; always the cooling rushing wind, and the shrill hiss of ski upon snow. Above us towers the Merced Range, wave upon wave of lofty stone glittering in the low winter sun. A huge ledge lifts suddenly on the curved face of the hill; we turn in a bright mist of ski-spun snow and slant anew along the canyon wall. The mountains soar higher into the flaming sky and the blue depths rise to enfold us as we skim down through the dusk to the shadowed valley with the swiftness known only to the ski."

Snowfields at Tuolumne Meadows.

On the snow-covered mountains of Yosemite, Mary Curry Tresidder reigned as queen of the slopes—a true ski pioneer.

The daughter of David and Jennie Curry, owners of the Curry Camping Company, she relished the opportunity to engage Yosemite's four seasons, and to share those experiences with the company's guests.

Mary and her husband Don were both dedicated to the outdoors. Their shared desire was to make Yosemite the "Switzerland of the West," and she loved the backcountry even more than he.

Mary particularly liked the high open slopes of 11,750-foot Mount Hoffman, making the demanding climb and exhilarating descents many times. Of those runs she wrote in the *British Ski Year Book* in the early 1930s, "Then came the reward of our labors, if the noble prospect and the intangibles of mount-climbing had not been enough. To our left lay what had been a glacial cirque and was now a great amphitheater of perfect snow, opening at the far end into a long, clear, rather steep

Mary made frequent use of the Snow Creek, Tenaya Lake and Tuolumne Meadows cabins, spending more than one hundred wintry nights at Snow Creek in the early 1930s. The backcountry beckoned in the summer, too.

Ski school director Jules Fritsch does a kickturn before heading downhill.

slope. No trees, no rocks marred the white surface. Without further ado, we swooped down and across the basin, glided from side to side of it, turned to any angle. It was exhilarating, hilarious. We rejoiced in the speed of our skis; we exulted as a strong man to run a race. Never have I known such moments. It was a terrestrial 'Ride of the Valkyries'; most of us found that we were indeed children of earth instead of heaven, and had perforce to renew our contact with terra firma now and again, but, ever so, it was bliss—bliss then to be alive; to be on skis was heaven!

"Fritsch, our Swiss guide, was in his element. Away he darted, leaving a series of S-turns down the mountainside, in the drop to May Lake, nearly 2,000 feet below. By the time the rest of us glided out across it, breathless, our knees were rather wobbly, but we had seen the glories of the world.... We all decided that if or when a cabin was built at May Lake, we would move in for the winter and climb up twice daily to the point below the cornice ... here was room for many a long day."

Even though Mary Tresidder loved the Snow Creek ski cabin and its splendid setting, it was closed at the end of the 1933-34 season after four years of disappointing returns. The closure marked one of Don Tresidder's few setbacks in establishing Yosemite as a year-round destination resort. Too few were ready for the rigors that went with ski touring in the wide-open spaces of the high country, particularly the long arduous climb out of the Valley.

Years later, Mary said that while Badger Pass may have been profitable, she didn't like giving up the idea of ski touring as a major attraction, a sport she preferred to downhill skiing. "Winter sports seemed to give some hope of spreading a thin layer of guests over the lean days. We were more hopeful than that, as a matter of fact. We had ourselves been infected by the deadly ski virus, and we saw Yosemite with its background of beauty as an outstanding winter place. We confidently expected that within a few years the High Sierra Camps would be a series of winter huts like those in the Alps or the Tyrol, with skiers touring from one to another. We found,

Ranger L. W. Emmont at Dana Meadows near Tioga Pass, 1933.

Don Tresidder shows off his telemark enroute to Tuolumne Meadows.

however, that people at that time did not know enough either about skiing or ski mountaineering to make that dream workable and, by the time they knew more about skiing, the lift type of sport had pushed ski touring far to the rear."

The Sierra Club formed its own winter sports committee, chaired by Ansel Adams and including ski mountaineers Orland Bartholomew, Bestor Robinson, David Brower and Otto Steiner. The club envisioned a program that would encourage "winter trips and exploration of the Sierra Nevada backcountry." For them, like Mary Tresidder, ski touring defined skiing. It was, as she observed, "the ultimate reason for skiing." They preferred the unrivaled freedom of the Yosemite high country and its miles of open slopes. Even Dr. Joel Hildebrand of the University of California and the father of four competitive downhill skiers, often spurned the growing crowds at Badger Pass, urging skiers to get away from "the merry-go-round of packed slopes and ski tows."

David Brower got his start as a renowned environmentalist while working as a publicist for the Yosemite Park & Curry Company in the mid 1930s. His sense of stewardship for the Earth began during those early days when he and Don Tresidder strived to make Yosemite a year-round destination.

When he was not working, Brower was out exploring the wonders of the park. On March 2, 1936, he joined four Sierra Club friends, Lewis Clark, Einar Nilsson, Boynton Kaiser and Bestor Robinson, to make the first winter ascent of 13,096-foot Mount Lyell, the highest point in the park.

Carrying fifty-pound packs and using sealskins on their skis, the adventurers were able to ski from Happy Isles up the snow-covered Vernal-Nevada Falls Trail to Little Yosemite Valley. They pressed on, reaching the ranger cabin at Merced Lake after sunset. "We were too exhausted to fix dinner," recalled Brower. On the following day, the group climbed to the headwaters of the Maclure Fork, establishing camp in the snow at "Hell Hole," nearly 2,000 feet above Bernice Lake.

Heavy wind complicated setting up tents and blew one down during the night. As they began their climb the next morning, the gale occasionally knocked one of them over, even when braced against the wind with a ski pole. "Long snow banners were flung far to the leeward of the peaks and arêtes, and in order not to follow suit while crossing the first spur of Mount Maclure, the men were forced to take off their skis and crawl, digging in hands and toes for anchorage," wrote Brower.

They crossed the second ridge to the Lyell Glacier and were able to reach its top. From there they climbed without skis up a 60 to 70 degree slope of snow and rock. The topmost rocks had been swept clear of snow, and the summit cairn was reached by midafternoon. There was no wind. They could see from the Sweetwater Mountains and northern Yosemite's Tower Peak to the Kaweah Peaks on the headwaters of the Kern.

Leaving the summit, they descended nearly 7,000 feet down to the Merced Lake ranger cabin and cups of steaming soup in front of the fireplace at midnight.

David Brower left Yosemite after a few years. During World War II, he joined the ski troops of the 10th Mountain Division and saw combat in Italy. He wrote and edited the *Manual of Ski Mountaineering*. After the war he was editor of the University of California Press. He served for seventeen years as the first executive director of the Sierra Club and later founded Friends of the Earth and Earth Island Institute, two environmental organizations whose influence has extended around the world. In 1998 Brower was awarded the Blue Planet Award by the Japanese government, one of the world's most prestigious environmental awards. It was for him, he noted, a trail of stewardship and service that originated in Yosemite.

David Brower and his mountaineering friends made the first winter ascents of 11,522-foot Mount Clark in the distance and 13,096-foot Mount Lyell.

Although the hut system envisioned by the Tresidders was never built, ski touring from Badger Pass became quite popular. Sentinel Dome, one of Yosemite's prime landmarks, was a favorite destination. Its steep, protected north face afforded excellent snow and skiing. A marked ski trail ran from the Glacier Point Mountain House to the dome. Walter Mosauer, an early ski coach for the University of California at Los Angeles, saw Sentinel Dome as perhaps the best ski run on the south rim. Over time, it became something of a "must-do," attracting many advanced skiers.

Bill Cahow, then a ski instructor at Badger Pass, recalled the time in 1939 when he and a half dozen of his Fresno friends headed up the Glacier Point Road for the distant dome. After admiring the world-class view from the summit, they headed down the slope in a series of linked turns through the feather-light snow. After dropping several hundred feet, most of the group pulled off to the side and stopped.

Cahow and Ted Goth, who now lives in Lodi, California, continued on. "It was fantastic skiing,"

Walter Mosauer skiing on Sentinel Dome with El Capitan in the background. Is it any wonder that there were thoughts in the early 1930s of building a tram to Glacier Point to provide easy access to these slopes?

reminisced Cahow. "A half dozen of us started at the top, but only the two of us got all the way down until we ran out of snow, perhaps a thousand feet vertical. We never got to the place where Sentinel Dome drops off to the valley. It was exciting skiing—no, it was great but stupid skiing. It took us nearly two hours to climb back up the hillside, and then we still had to ski all the way back to Badger Pass."

Bill Cahow and his friends on Sentinel Dome with Yosemite Falls beyond.

In the late 1920s, a young German skier, Otto Steiner, left his native Bavaria and made his way to the United States, finally settling in Stockton, California. He worked for a company that was trying to develop a salt water barrier for the San Joaquin River delta. Along the way he lived at Lake Placid, New York, forerunning the race courses for the 1932 Winter Olympic Games and participating in cross-country races against some of the top Nordic skiers.

Otto made numerous ski forays into the Sierra's high country when, as he recalled, there was comparatively little skiing going on. In 1932, he went alone on a trans-Sierra ski crossing—only because he couldn't find anyone to go along. His passion for skiing never waned and he helped hundreds of beginners to ski, often taking an entire club on a ski outing.

"I worked for Don and Mary Tresidder a couple of years, trying to push cross-country skiing," Steiner related. "I found some wonderful slopes in the Clark Range just fifteen miles from Glacier Point. But by that time they had decided on Badger Pass. They wanted me to be the manager there, but I didn't want anything to do with that crowded little ski slope."

I saw him last in the 1980s, when he stopped by my Fresno office for a short visit. He was enroute to the Sierra from his retirement home in Walnut Creek. On the top of his car, the 80-year-young skier had an immaculate pair of laminated wooden skis, equipped with old cable bindings. He was headed up again to the slopes above Glacier Point. And he was going alone. Once again, he couldn't find anyone to join him.

"Otto," I asked, "Aren't you worried about going up there alone?"

"I can take care of myself. But if not, can you think of a better place to die?" he asked with a twinkle in his eye.

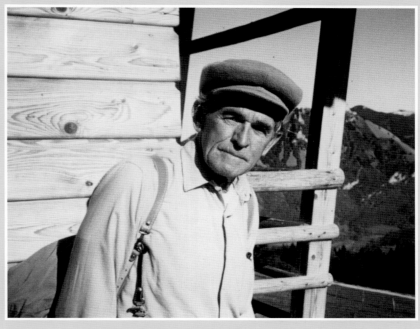

Courtesy of Otto Steiner

Otto Steiner, grand old man of the mountains, taken in the Bavarian Alps in 1976.

Courtesy of Carson White

Skiers at Glacier Point in the 1960s.

In January 1941, the Sno-Motor was introduced to haul skiers to the Glacier Point Mountain House. A strange contraption resembling nothing but itself, it was described by one skier as a "tank-like vehicle with a single tread that pulls a sled. It is gas powered and has a cab for the driver. About fifteen skiers and their equipment can be comfortably carried."

Publicist Ben Tarnutzer recalled one early trip in the Sno-Motor. "In midafternoon we again donned ski boots, climbed into our snow-going gondola, and started up the road. We wanted to learn whether it would negotiate a really stiff grade in such soft snow, so when we reached the junction of the Sentinel Dome spur, the driver headed it directly against the bank. It gave a shudder and a snort and with a mighty heave was over the top. Gabe Goldsworthy gave such a squeal of delight that the driver in consternation stopped the motor. Finding no one in distress, he started it again, and to our astonishment, the sled moved right up the grade from a dead stop."

During the second half of the 1930s, the National Park Service

The Sno-Motor reminded Ben Tarnutzer of the lumberjack who saw a donkey engine in operation and remarked in admiration, "She ain't much for looks, but she's hell for strong."

began to debate the appropriate winter uses of the park. In 1940, the Yosemite Committee on Winter Activity was organized to help the service formulate a policy. Led by Dr. Joel Hildebrand and with the help of Bestor Robinson and Frank Wentworth, all serious skiers and members of the Sierra Club, the committee wanted a hut and trail system, recognizing that "ski touring is the most appropriate type of winter use for the national parks, since it makes available the scenic grandeur for which the national parks were created."

Still looking for a ski hut site in the backcountry, Mary and Don Tresidder camped overnight in the snow in May 1938 at the foot of Horizon Ridge near Ostrander Lake. Mary later wrote, "We reached Glacier Point just at sunset in an eerie glory I shall never forget, crimson spreading from the Sierra Nevada peaks across the deep canyon of the Merced River to the snow at our very feet. The next day we skied by way of Illilouette Ridge to Ostrander Lake and back, a trip that took us from dawn until long after dark. That was years before the Ostrander Ski Hut was built, but it gave us a

foretaste of its terrain. We skied back to the Valley the day after that, along the Pohono Trail, and I had my first look at that exciting slope above Inspiration Point.... Those were long days, but there was magic in them, as there is today for those who venture forth on skis."

The real issues were how many and what kind of huts to have. The Sierra Club wanted a simple, spartan shelter, and more than one. From their experience with the Snow Creek chalet, the Tresidders knew their guests would demand more than a common room. The park service worried about cost. Finally, a single, two-story shelter at Ostrander Lake, about eight miles southeast of Badger Pass, was agreed upon. Using the labors of the Civilian Conservation Corps, the project moved forward quickly. By January 1941, the hut was ready for business.

An instant hit among ski mountaineers, the hut offered accommodations for twenty-five skiers, with women occupying the second floor. There was no charge for those who brought in their own food and bedding.

Ostrander Ski Hut in the late 1940s. From the left are Lew Butler, Lucy Butler, an unknown friend, Mary Curry Tresidder, William D. Grishaw and Nick Clinch.

OSTRANDER SKI HUT

Late in that first season, the company sent Ben Tarnutzer and a film crew to the Ostrander hut. He wrote in the *Western Ski Annual,* "It being mid April, we had fully expected to find spring snow. Instead, to our surprise, we found dry powder snow of a quality that was nothing short of perfect, and as you all know, powder snow is the delight of all photographers.

"There were only one or two ski tracks to be seen in that whole region, made by skiers who had been there the week previous. These were soon erased by a fresh fall of powder snow, which gave us a four-inch surface with which to work. To complete our happiness, the sun came out and shone brightly, beautiful cumulus clouds rolled in to decorate an intense blue sky, and snow plumes trailed the skiers on every run.

"It was thrilling to watch our best skiers swing down the slopes in a series of precision ski maneuvers, only equaled by their spectacular schusses down to the lake, taken at the terrific speed that the steepness of the ride made possible... We spent a solid week taking pictures at Ostrander Lake, and even at the end we were sorry to leave."

Later, Charley Proctor recalled that Luggi Foeger and Jules Fritsch thought "the skiing [at Ostrander Hut] was so good that they had died and gone to skier's heaven."

Relaxing in front of the Ostrander Ski Hut.

After the Second World War, the snowbound Glacier Point Mountain House again became a popular destination. From 1948 to 1966, George and Dorothy Mayer had the pleasure—and the perils—of working as winter caretakers. The two veteran travelers and adventurers from England survived frozen pipes and were often without power or running water. The Glacier Point Hotel itself was closed, but the Mountain House was open and could accommodate more than a hundred people. On special occasions in the Valley, such as the Winter Club's skating parties at the Curry Rink, the Mayers would touch off a spectacular firefall of burning embers. There is a large painting of the winter firefall by Dorothy in the park museum.

The Mountain House with its awe-inspiring vista point attracted a steady flow of adventurous skiers who made the strenuous eleven-mile trek from Badger Pass seeking the sublime grandeur of Yosemite's snow-covered high country. Later the park service plowed the road to the top of the Glacier Point switchbacks, allowing visitors to drive that far and then ski or snowshoe down to the point.

The Mayer's wintry Shangri-la came to a sad end in 1966 when George was injured and had to be rescued by park rangers. The Mayers reluctantly concluded that the rigors of the job were too much at their age and did not return the following season. During the summer of 1969, the Glacier Point Hotel and Mountain House were destroyed by fire, concluding a rich and colorful chapter of Yosemite's history.

Luggi Foeger, sitting in the Weasel, with Badger Pass skiers on a visit to Ostrander Hut.

View from the window of the Glacier Point Mountain House.

Over the past three decades, cross-country skiing has come full circle. In the days before the runs at Chinquapin and Badger Pass were opened, ski touring around the Valley with a occasional trip into the backcountry was what most skiers did. In 1969, the Curry Company tapped veteran mountaineer and former park ranger Wayne Merry to head the new Yosemite Mountaineering School. An expert mountaineer and climber with "big wall" experience, he participated in the first successful ascent of El Capitan in 1958. He had worked for the National Park Service for ten years, most recently as chief ranger at Mount McKinley National Park. He was accomplished on "skinny skis" and an expert in the difficult art of waxing. And like Nic Fiore, Wayne was a people person, capable of instilling confidence in his pupils.

"When I first started the school, I suggested to (then Vice President) Bob Maynard that we start a cross-country ski school, too. He wouldn't hear of it the first year, but the second year he agreed that it was time. Through Bob's skiing connections, he located Ned Gillette and Jim Speck to be the first instructors, and they were great choices. They had been on the U.S. Nordic Ski Team," Wayne recalled. "Bob gave me a pretty free hand and complete support. The only thing he insisted on was that I hire Loyd Price and try him out as chief guide. I did, and it worked out well. He was a good organizer, really safe, and tremendously energetic."

Wayne's summer programs urged visitors to "go climb a rock." But with the arrival of winter, he turned to cross-country skiing and ski mountaineering in the wide-open expanses of Yosemite's backcountry. With the thrills came danger, so the school held classes in winter survival, teaching its charges how to build snow caves and survive a storm if caught in the open.

Wayne formed an alliance with The North Face, an emerging Bay Area retailer and manufacturer of mountain equipment. Working with The North Face, the school offered advanced and adventurous skiers a combination of ski touring and snow camping, followed by an afternoon of downhill skiing at Badger Pass.

While *Ski Racing* headlined the new programs, veteran sports writer Omer Crane of the *Fresno Bee,* long familiar with the Yosemite ski scene, predicted that Merry's efforts to push nordic skiing would go the way of the Tresidder's Snow Creek chalet. "The skiers won't give up their chairlifts. Downhill skiers might give cross-country a try, but it's too much like work. They are glued to the seats of their chairlift."

The initial response almost confirmed Crane's prediction. Merry's first promotional effort focused on the downhill ski clubs and it flopped. "Then we went for the back-to-nature people who saw cross-country as a means of getting into the backcountry in winter—I was one myself— and it took off like a rocket," said Merry. New trails were marked, with the Dewey Point Trail emerging as a favorite.

Wayne Merry.

Good press coverage followed. Ski newspapers, such as the *Far West Ski News*, described Yosemite as "the best place in the West for ski touring." And despite the masochist image, a new generation of hardy winter sports enthusiasts began digging snow caves and testing themselves.

Wayne recounted how he promoted the revived sport. "In 1972 I suggested that if we could do a really sensational cross-country wilderness trip somewhere in the world, we could use it as a marketing tool for Yosemite. I got together Jack Miller, Jed Williamson and Ned Gillette, and we decided to ski from Bettles on the Arctic Circle in Alaska up to Prudhoe Bay, just before the pipeline was started. We did—well, we didn't. We got across the Brooks Range, took one look at the flat Arctic slope and back at those awesome mountains, and voted to turn back and climb rather than go to the ocean. Ned was really furious, but later, on top of a fantastic peak, he agreed we had been right. And of course that was his launching pad to a whole career of expeditions. The North Face made our equipment to order and we did the photos for their

Wayne Merry strides through the forest.

Ned Gillette, on the left, had been on the U.S. Nordic Ski Team. He joins Wayne Merry, Don Mossman and Jim Speck as they warm up for the Nordic Holiday Race.

catalogue that year. And we used the slide talk all over California to promote cross-country, and it really took off. Very shortly we had several hundred pairs of rental skis, and up to ten instructors going at once on weekends."

"I consciously tried to get cross-country skiing going because I loved it and thought other people would. The time was ripe and people were ready for it," he recalled. For the first time ever, cross-country skis with lignostone edges and three-pin bindings could be purchased in the park and in neighboring metropolitan areas. In 1972 Merry launched the first cross-country race since the war called the Nordic Holiday Race at Summit Meadows up Glacier Point Road from Badger Pass. "At the first one we had sixty registrants. It exploded from there and became around four hundred which was about as many as could be handled out of Badger. We had some fine after-ski parties, with prizes for all sorts of categories." By the time the season wound down, the National Park Service estimated that 30,000 skiers had hit the nordic trail.

Wayne remembers that "Yosemite was the first such school in cross-country, but got passed up pretty fast because we couldn't use machinery to groom ski trails except at Badger. We had to foot-pack all our ski trails." His biggest challenge was finding qualified cross-country ski instructors. "The only ones we could find were Norwegian college students at Berkeley. We had some terrible fights with the immigration authorities who insisted that citizen ski instructors were a dime a dozen in the states. For a while, I thought they had us stopped. We finally won that argument, and we had a good bunch of instructors who would come up on weekends."

Merry touched the young and old alike. "I'll always remember that when we first started the cross-country school an old man walked into the shop, which was then part of the dress store in Yosemite Lodge. He wore a double-breasted coat, pork pie hat and knickers. Had fragile looking legs. His name was Ottmar Friz, a port captain at the Oakland seaport. I think he was seventy-five then. He wanted to take cross-country lessons. I asked him if he had ever skied

The start of a big race.

The cross-country skiing instructors at the Yosemite Mountaineering School in 1989.

before. He said 'yes'—when he was a kid in Europe, when skis were about eleven feet long and there was one great long pole. The situation scared me to death but he signed up for instruction. He never got the long graceful glide, but he just stayed with it and brought his wife up not long after. He said one time, 'You've given me a new lease on life!' He entered the Nordic Holiday Race several times. Always sidestepped down the tough hills—and always came in about last. He loved it to pieces, and got the Oldest Competitor prize for several years. Wonderful man. We all just loved him."

One of the sidelines of the mountaineering school was YOSAR, the park's search and rescue unit. "At the time, there were few park rangers who could climb well enough to do rescues in Yosemite," Wayne recalled. "So they called the Mountaineer School guides every time there was a tough one. We were glad to do it but it was wrecking the business. So I talked to Jim Bridwell, who was sort of the spokesman for Camp 4 which was open all winter, and we went over to see Keith Neilson, the assistant

superintendent. I suggested that a group of top climbers be given unlimited camping time in Camp 4, provided that half of them were available at any one time for rescues. When they were called, they would be signed up as a rescue team. It worked."

Overnight ski trips to Glacier Point became a big hit, with skiers bedding down in the seasonally vacated gift shop. Skiers ventured into the Tuolumne Grove from Crane Flat and up the Tioga Road. Soon others were pushing beyond Ostrander Lake and Glacier Point. They began venturing out to the Clark Range, making trans-Sierra trips and crossing both Donohue and Tioga Passes.

With the return of cross-country skiing, Mary and Don Tresidder's long cherished dream of Yosemite as a ski mountaineering mecca had become reality, although backcountry ski huts were not to be. The Yosemite Mountaineering School brought a new vision and approach to winter sports in the park. Even the National Park Service waxed enthusiastically over cross-country skiing. "Yosemite will be one of the major touring centers in the Far West with the finest nordic school in the country," superintendent Les Amberger had predicted. And, of course, he was right on.

A quiet moment at Glacier Point.

Backcountry use was not just for cross-country skiers. The National Park Service inaugurated free snowshoe walks as part of its interpretive activities, led by rangers Jon Kinney and Warren White. Dog sledders and snowmobilers began using the snow-covered roads. Campers and recreational vehicles were accommodated in the Valley. During peak weekends and holidays, occupancy in the campgrounds rivaled the busy summer season.

By the early 1960s, snowmobilers had reached the high country of Yosemite, where they found such beautiful sites as Dana and Tuolumne Meadows superb winter playgrounds. Frozen, snow-blanketed lakes beckoned. There were few restrictions. One brave soul reportedly managed to reach the top of 11,000-foot Donohue Pass. On another occasion a group from Lee Vining crossed on the Tioga Road to Crane Flat where they were picked up by friends and delivered to the Ahwahnee Hotel for the night before returning home the next day.

Snowshoers gaze up at a giant in the Mariposa Grove of Big Trees.

Veteran ranger Ron Mackie remembers that the snowmobiles were perceived as just another use of the park with few questioning their impact. That is until the passage of the National Wilderness Act of 1964 when their use was restricted to the Tioga and Glacier Point Roads.

As backcountry use grew, there were inevitable conflicts between skiers and snowshoers on the one hand and snowmobilers on the other. The biggest objection was to the noise in the otherwise pristine wilderness. Snowmobilers claimed their impact was minimal and that, with a little common courtesy, there was room enough for everyone. The verbal sparring continued and there were unconfirmed reports of occasional fights. After several winters of controversy, superintendent Amberger finally decided to ban snowmobiling entirely in 1974.

With increased winter use of the high country and to implement the ban on snowmobiling, chief ranger Bill Wendt decided that there was a need for a park service presence at Tuolumne Meadows. Jeff Mathis was the first ranger to winter over, and a long line followed, including Randy and Judy Morgenson, Marilyn Muse and Jim Harper, Anne and Chas MacQuarie. For six isolated months their main assignment was to provide information and assistance to passing skiers and other winter visitors. They also assisted in snow surveys and search and rescue operations. In January 1982, the MacQuaries skied out to rescue a nearly frozen young boy, Donnie Priest, from the snow-covered wreckage of his parents' airplane atop the crest of the Sierra.

Veteran rangers still talk about Squaw Valley climber and skier Rick Sylvester's effort to turn El Capitan into one gigantic ski jump. In a clandestine, 1972 effort to obtain some dramatic footage for the movie, *Infinity of Crystals*, Sylvester fashioned a snow ramp on the lip of the famed monolith. Zooming off into space, he dropped down his "3,000-foot fall

Courtesy of Lynn Moss

Trans-Sierra skiers at Tioga Pass in 1989.

line," kicking off his skis using a special release mechanism. He popped his parachute and began a descent to the Valley below. But somewhere along the way things went wrong. Instead of landing in the open El Capitan Meadow, Sylvester ended up rather unceremoniously in the trees. And worse yet, the camera he carried malfunctioned. While another camera captured the descent, Sylvester got none of the dramatic footage he had worked so hard for. To add insult to injury, park rangers soon arrived on the scene, citing him for making an illegal jump and nailing his film crew for not having secured the necessary commercial filming permit.

© Chris Falkenstein

Dave Page on the first nordic ski descent of the Ledge Trail from Glacier Point in 1989.

The Ledge Trail down from Glacier Point had a formidable and, at times, deadly reputation, particularly among summer hikers. It had been carved out of the rugged, northwest face of Glacier Point, dropping in a series of sharp switchbacks to the Valley below. Over the years, it had claimed the lives of several hikers and finally was closed to public use in the late 1950s.

Winter use of the trail was another matter, however. Old skiers' tales persist that adventurers had attempted the route after World War II. But the first known descent on skis of the near vertical trail is recalled by the one living survivor of that semi-suicidal run, a 3,000-foot fall line with almost no room for lateral movement.

"It must have been 1972," recalls retired park ranger Pete Thompson who, along with Leroy Rust, pushed their skis over the lip of Glacier Point that spring day. "As I recall, it was Rusty's idea. From his office at the post office in Yosemite Valley he could look right up there and see the ribbon of snow that lined the trail. That's where it started.

"We looked it over and decided it was doable—that it would be a good challenge," Thompson recalled. "We had a couple of friends spot for us from the Valley, in case we got into trouble. Once we started down there was no turning back. The snow was as hard as granite. We could hear the water running under the snow as we moved down. We didn't do much turning. It wasn't so much skiing as one long sideslip. We managed to make it down, but it was all I could muster."

"Wild" and "unbelievable" only begin to describe some of the extreme action that has transpired since that first descent. Blessed with some of the most dramatic terrain in the country, the high peaks of Yosemite have become a proving ground for cutting-edge skiers. Much like the big walls that have lured climbers to Yosemite for seventy years, snow-filled chutes, couloirs, gullies and other sheer slabs have drawn thrill seekers. Some of the runs could well be named "Death Wish" or "Suicide."

Perhaps the most daring feat occurred in 1980 when Eric Perlman and Bob Bellman skied down the cable route of Half Dome and lived to tell about it. Getting up the ice-shrouded cableway was tough enough, requiring two attempts. Getting down was hair raising. After gaining the summit of the famed landmark, the two adventurers put on their skis and faced down the snow-covered, convex-shaped dome—the outer limit of skiing. Maintaining control of their chattering skis was a big problem. "The toughest part came in the transition area where the snow gave way to ice and then bare rock,"

explains Perlman. By using ice axes they had lashed to their ski poles, they managed to work their way around this problem area and then ski down the rest of the way, avoiding the nearly sheer western face.

In the early 1970s, with the spring opening of the Tioga Road, a handful of downhill skiers trekked to the summit of Mount Dana for hard won spring skiing. In succeeding winters, the Yosemite Association, a nonprofit organization that benefits the National Park Service, offered winter tours. Participants were airlifted to Lee Vining and then skied over Tioga Pass to Yosemite Valley.

Federal Magistrate Don Pitts and his wife Kay often led ski tours to Glacier Point, Ostrander Lake and other sections of the park for the Winter Club. The highlight of each season was a week-long, trans-Sierra trek over Tioga Pass. Food and fuel were cached at selected points along the way to ease the load. "We had some great outings," Kay Pitts recalls.

Wayne Merry left Yosemite in 1974 for new challenges at Atlin,

British Columbia, and on the mountaineering circuit. His successful programs had opened the park to the kind of activities that many felt were more in keeping with a wilderness area.

After Wayne's departure, Loyd Price took over the climbing school while former Olympian Ned Gillette headed the cross-country operations. Gillette moved on three years later, returning east to Stowe, Vermont, where he ran the famed Trapp Family Lodge. Price then assumed responsibility for the entire school operation as well as other guest activities. He set out to reinvigorate both the summer and winter programs. He launched a successful rafting program for the summer visitor and convinced the park service to allow grooming of the Glacier Point Road, which immensely aided ski touring. Along the way, he became the first American ski instructor to be certified in both alpine and nordic ski techniques.

Ice climbing was added to the program. Using a new curved ice axe and ice screws, Price and his advanced students climbed some of the park's fabled waterfalls that had frozen over during the coldest

part of the winter. "There had been some ice climbing earlier, but the sport made some real progress after the Mountaineering School arrived," he recalled. "When freezing weather permitted, the ice climbers would clamber up the frozen form of Sentinel Falls or several smaller falls west of Leaning Tower."

In the winter of 1985, the unassuming Price teamed up with Bruce Brossman and Chris Falkenstein to make a one-day trans-Sierra crossing. The three met the night before in the lounge of the Mountain Room in Yosemite Lodge to complete their final preparations. Early the next morning they flew to Lee Vining. Donning skis at the snowline in Lee Vining Canyon, they made the long and laborious climb to Tioga Pass. Following the easy and welcomed descent to Tuolumne Meadows, they pushed on past Tenaya Lake to descend the Snow Creek Trail. Around dusk, the weary travelers arrived in Yosemite Valley. The spent Price, senior of the three, retired to his bed for some well earned rest. Soon his wife Debbie came home and reported that Brossman and Falkenstein were in the bar at the same place as they had met the night before. Forevermore their trans-Sierra trek became known as the "Bar-to-Bar Ski Trip."

The Ostrander Hut finally came into its own in the early 1970s. For many of its early years, the hut had been a disappointment to the Curry Company. Bunk counts were low and revenues often failed to meet expenses. Even attempts to boost overnight use by transporting clientele with Weasels, the war surplus snow vehicles, did little to stem the red ink. In any event, the Weasels came under heavy fire from skiers, and their use was discontinued in the late 1960s. Soon after, the company terminated its interest in the hut. Left with no alternative, the park service took over in 1969, placing a ranger on site to provide an official presence but little more.

However, things changed quickly as the new programs of the Mountaineering School took hold. With renewed interest in ski touring by the Yosemite Winter Club and the mountaineering section of the Sierra Club, the use of the Ostrander Hut soared. By 1974 the park service could no longer handle the load and

the Yosemite Association took over, installing Howard Weamer, a longtime Yosemite lover, as hut keeper. Howard and his charges skied over large areas of the Clark Range and Buena Vista crest. Even during the drought years, the hut remained popular. Several adventurous souls carried their ice skates in and used the frozen surface of Ostrander Lake as a rink. Today, the hut is so popular that reservations must be made far in advance for weekends.

These cross-country skiers are "skating" along the groomed trail on Glacier Point Road.

Courtesy of Lynn Moss

Ice-skating amid the magnificent surroundings at Ostrander Lake in 1992.

HOWARD WEAMER

At first glance Howard Weamer has the appearance of a modern-day mountain man. Bearded, lean and lanky, Howard eschews many of the trappings of our fast-paced life. Serving as the caretaker at the Ostrander Hut for the past twenty-five winters, he has helped others enjoy the Yosemite backcountry and the adventures that come with cross-country skiing.

Howard has explored many of the remote sections of the park in winter, reveling in its snow-clad mantle. Along the way, he has taken some of the finest photos to come out of his Yosemite world. As with all fine photographers, Howard feels with his eyes and his soul, perceiving forms, shapes and the variations of lighting that may escape the rest of us. Even now, after years of looking across snow-covered Ostrander Lake, he still sees new variations of that wintry theme. He has written extensively about the remote ski hut and the backcountry, capturing its colorful history in his own publication, *The Perfect Art.*

Weamer has also known the grim side of Yosemite winter. In 1981, he was airlifted from the hut for emergency medical care. Three years later, on his first trip of the season, he temporarily lost his way in a blinding blizzard. When night fell, he found himself without a flashlight. Eventually, he stumbled upon another lost party, and with their light found a marker that enabled them to reach the hut. It was, he noted, his "Trip to Hell."

As with John Muir, who knew skiing as poetry in motion, Weamer sees skiing as something of an art form, combining a measure of sport, a bit of pantheism, a special world of visual dynamics and some serious living thrown in.

Photograph by Art Baggett, Jr.

Howard Weamer stands in the door of the Ostrander Ski Hut.

Across the Sierra the snowpack in the winter of 1982-83 exceeded all past measurements. As spring unfolded, skiers went wild. Long before the trans-Sierra Tioga Road was open, they made their way into the high country. Many focused on Mount Dana. Here they found skiing as few had ever experienced. Although ski pioneer Jules Fritsch and other members of his staff had climbed to Dana's imposing 13,000-foot summit on skis in the late 1920s, they never challenged its steepest routes.

For Tom Carter, Chris Cox, Alan Barg, Chris Falkenstein and others with ties to the Mountaineering School and Yosemite's search and rescue team, this was a ski mountaineer's dream come true. They plunged down chutes and slopes with a vengeance, tempting themselves with the most difficult and challenging runs they could find. They ranged over much of the Tioga Pass and Saddlebag Lake areas, making one ski conquest after another. Today, Carter, an early ski instructor with the Mountaineering School and later with Ned Gillette at Stowe, only smiles when he talks about the "good old days" of that period, when he and Barg made

numerous ski descents of the big mountains on nordic skis, including the mind-boggling trip down the couloir on Mount Dana.

With the passage of the California Wilderness Act by Congress in 1984, almost ninety-five percent of Yosemite National Park was set aside as wilderness. Otto Steiner's dream of a network of ski chalets in the Yosemite high country had disappeared forever. But for backcountry skiers and winter mountaineers aided by new equipment, this made little difference.

Carter is quick to point out that today there is a new generation of ski mountaineers in the high country who are "doing ski things that are unbelievable." There is a mental attitude that nothing is impossible. Much like the distance runners who continue to set faster records, each additional extreme skiing accomplishment raises the bar for others to challenge. For them, any slope, no matter how steep or intimidating, is skiable as long as it holds snow and is wide enough to accommodate a skier. With some of the most challenging terrain in the world, Yosemite has become a new proving ground.

© Chris Falkenstein

Tim Messick, in a first descent of Mount Conness on nordic skis.

© Chris Falkenstein

A snowboarder descends the slopes of Mount Dana.

129

At the end of the big winter of 1992-93, Glen Poulsen, son of Squaw Valley founder and ski pioneer Wayne Poulsen, streaked across the Sierra on skis in what may well be record time. Leaving Mammoth Mountain at daybreak, Poulsen sped up the San Joaquin River canyon, crossed Minaret Pass, Island Pass and then 11,000-foot Donohue Pass. From there he schussed down Lyell Canyon to the Tioga Road and through Tuolumne Meadows to Tenaya Lake, then down Snow Creek to his Yosemite Valley destination. In the space of about nine hours, the marathon mountaineer had skied nearly sixty miles while climbing almost 3,000 feet and then descending nearly twice that enroute to the Valley. Poulsen dismissed the heroics of his blazing ski trip. "It was fun. I enjoyed doing it," he said somewhat modestly.

Seventy years have passed since Orland Bartholomew's epic solo trek up the spine of the Sierra Nevada. On April 28, 1999, four of Yosemite's modern-day backcountry titans, Howard Weamer, Tim Messick, Art Baggett and his son Fritz, arrived in Yosemite Valley, after replicating

Courtesy of Art Baggett, Jr.

Howard Weamer, Fritz and Art Baggett and Tim Messick arrive tired and happy at Mirror Lake in the Valley.

the original journey. While others have skied the same general route over the years, the four used Bartholomew's diary to accurately follow his trail.

Their twenty-eight-day adventure began with threatening weather, and by the end of the first day a fierce spring snowstorm blew across the crest engulfing them. It wasn't just a one-day affair either—it continued unabated for eight days out of their first eleven

on the trail. One night about two feet of snow an hour accumulated outside their tents, forcing them to shovel at regular intervals. Even with the snowstorms, however, they were able to accomplish the entire journey in twenty-eight days instead of the three-and-a-half months that it took Bartholomew.

Art Baggett commented, "They hadn't even invented the parallel turn in Bart's day. We were able to use jump turns, parallel turns and

even get some air, as Fritz did down the chute on Mount Whitney. We benefitted from seventy years of advances in ski technique and equipment, allowing us to ski slopes Bart was forced to walk down."

Unlike Bartholomew, who received very little press coverage of his trip, modern technology followed this latest venture. The *Fresno Bee* created a website for the trip and gave updates when available.

Art Baggett skiing the Golden Staircase below Palisade Lake and Mather Pass at 9,600 feet.

Howard Weamer looks out of his tent below Silver Pass at 10,800 feet.

Fritz Baggett descends the face at Mount Bago above Charlotte Lake in Sequoia National Park.

WHITNEY TO YOSEMITE
APRIL 1999

Crabtree Meadow below Mount Whitney.

Tim Messick and Fritz Baggett under Mount Lyell.

What's ahead on the Yosemite winter sports horizon for these men and a few women who push the limits of skiing? As many of today's mountaineers look into the crystal ball of the new future, they see some superb winters ahead. Tim Messick of Yosemite believes tomorrow's adventurers will push the bar even higher. "Skiing and all winter sports will just keep getting better; the equipment keeps getting better. People are in better shape and they want to get out there and get away from the crowds," he predicts. "The old perception that 'boarders can't go uphill' no longer holds." By using lighter and smaller snowshoes, they can climb almost any mountain, carrying their snowboards on their backs. Once on the summit, it's onto their boards and downhill thrills.

Doug Nidever of June Lake, another respected Sierra mountaineer, shares Messick's views. As he looks to the future of winter mountaineering, he sees major changes. He uses words like "explosive" and "quantum leap" to describe the anticipated changes

in Sierra mountaineering. He points to the breathtaking 6,000-foot descents made by snowboarders who are pushing the limit. Nidever talks about ice climbers who are tackling frozen waterfalls in places like Lee Vining Canyon. He speculates that in the not-too-distant future, skiers will be attempting a round-trip, trans-Sierra crossing in a twenty-four-hour period.

However, the Mountaineering School's Loyd Price doesn't see things moving quite so fast as Yosemite winter sports enters the new millennium. He is confident that Yosemite will retain its winter appeal to families and the general public simply because it is a national park. Reflecting the park service's mandate for preservation and protection, he suggests that "any change will be one of slow and steady continued growth."

Fritz Baggett catching air on the slopes above Crabtree Meadow below Mount Whitney.

In 1982, Galen Rowell and several friends made the winter trek from Mount Whitney to Yosemite.
Beneath the incomparable beauty of a moonlit night, they move across the Kern Plateau on the John Muir Trail.

THE MAGIC CONTINUES

© *Keith Walklet*

Global warming aside, winter will surely continue to be a yearly visitor to Yosemite. Like clockwork, the winds will blow energy-filled storms down from the Gulf of Alaska and, as the Sierra's steep flank forces the moisture-laden air upward, snow will fall. I was reminded of this during a recent return to Yosemite.

For this latest visit, a swift-moving arctic storm swept over California, spreading a white blanket that stretched even to the lower foothills. In all, a foot and a half of rare powder fell in Yosemite Valley, and I had the pleasure of being snowed in.

It was as if Mother Nature was encouraging me to stay in my former home just a little longer. A tempting thought, too. Nic Fiore's story came to mind. He arrived in the winter of 1948 and expected to return to Canada upon its conclusion. Now over fifty years later, he is still in Yosemite and has never looked back. And Nic's story is not uncommon for Yosemite residents. For me, one winter became fourteen and those winters remain the finest I can recall. Yosemite winters are different than what I was used to on the East Coast where the short days and biting air were to be endured, rather than enjoyed.

As I watched the tiny, wind-driven flakes accumulate, I thought of the hearty individuals that had "suffered" a similar fate through the years since Lamon first overwintered in Yosemite Valley. Clearing storms were my introduction to Yosemite's awesome winter weather but it was summer volunteering in the park service darkroom and subsequent jobs in the public relations department for the Curry Company and Yosemite Concession Services that introduced me to its history.

Figures in faded black and white photographs became real people to me. Most I would never know personally, but others, like Nic Fiore, David Brower and Rusty Rust, I did have the good fortune to spend time with. As John Muir once said, "Give a yank on something, and you'll find it hitched to everything else in the universe." They became my links with the past, and the energy, friendship and joy for life of these pioneers grew to be as great as the monumental cliffs and waterfalls of the Valley.

Geologists frequently remind us that we exist in a mere moment of time, but mix wonderful people into the equation—enthusiastic and unabashedly in love with the park's magnificent landscape—and the geologic sliver of time can expand to span generations. This book celebrates the exploits of those early winter enthusiasts, now gifts to future generations. It was the energy of such unselfish individuals that gave birth to "the Yosemite winter experience," and it is that type of energy that will be necessary to sustain its future.

Courtesy of Ann Grishaw Mosser

The Valley is crystal white after a fresh snowfall.
This was the Tresidders' 1935 Christmas card.

As joyous as Yosemite's winters have been, not everyone has unbridled enthusiasm with the growth of winter sports and facilities in the park. Beneath the park's winter blanket is the hard, cruel fact that the management of the natural resource and the facilities is ever-changing. The National Park Service is tasked with a dual mission: to protect the resource, unimpaired, for future generations and to make it available for public enjoyment.

Through the years, the pendulum has swung back and forth between the two issues. So it is that along with each and every aspect of the park facilities and services, the ice rink and Badger Pass have periodically been scrutinized with the same careful consideration for appropriateness.

The discussion has eased since the current Concession Services Plan was adopted in 1993. Both downhill skiing and ice-skating, for the time being, are approved services. But this status is subject to change by either the National Park Service or the concessionaire (with NPS approval).

The present concessionaire, Yosemite Concession Services, a subsidiary of Delaware North Company, has a fifteen-year contract that expires in 2008. The past few winters have been anything but kind to them. Floods, rock slides and government shutdowns have all conspired to keep YCS from offering a full season of skiing. Added to that mix of calamities has been the challenge of operating, at best, a stagnant business. The downhill ski industry, except for snowboarding, is not experiencing growth at Badger Pass or elsewhere. Still, the long-range goal is not only a healthy but also harmonious operation in Yosemite.

If the recent disasters have had a silver lining, it is that they have helped isolate the economic aspects of winter activities and offered a glimpse of their impact on the visitor and park community. The opportunities for experiences in the snow are diverse but it is clear that historic Badger Pass is the hub, the gateway to understanding of Yosemite's mysteries. Nic Fiore said, "There is simply no better place to learn to ski." I maintain that there is simply no better place to learn to love winter.

With discussion concluded for the time being and park management's endorsement that the winter experiences of the last seventy-odd years will continue, we can only ask if anyone in our generation can match the singular devotion that Yosemite's winter pioneers demonstrated, for that is the catalyst that translates facts, figures and words into legacies.

In some ways, the new generation of winter sports enthusiasts is driven by the ghost of earlier winter pioneers. Collectively they join that select band of men and women who chased the secrets of winter, the spirit of the snows. Whether alone or together, they seek to define the mysteries and magic that is a Yosemite winter.

They seek the same sense of adventure that sent Orland Bartholomew up against the snows of the mighty Sierra. They follow the trailblazing spirit of Jules Fritsch, Yosemite's first ski instructor. Others pursue the exhilaration that Mary Curry Tresidder knew in her ski flights to the high country. They long to discover the wonders Leroy Rust knew in his seventy-year love affair with the snow and ice of Yosemite. Perhaps unknowingly, snowboarders covet the freedom that led Otto Steiner to the remote snowfields. And still others, with or without skis, skates or snowboard—the conveyance is immaterial—seek the silence, the solemnity that winter bestows on this great natural cathedral, this sacred, magic place.

Keith Walklet, Boise, Idaho
May 1999

(Keith was Manager, Visitor Information and Media Services for Yosemite Concession Services until he moved to Boise in early 1999 to pursue his passion for photography.)

Yosemite Falls cascades into the Valley on a winter morning.

*Everybody needs beauty
as well as bread,
places to play in and pray in
where Nature may heal and cheer
and give strength
to body and soul alike.*

John Muir

INDEX

PHOTO CREDITS

OTHER BOOKS BY COLDSTREAM PRESS

What Shall We Do Tomorrow at Lake Tahoe by Ellie Huggins.
A complete activities guide for Lake Tahoe, Carson Pass and Truckee

The fourth edition of this 320-page guide to the year-round recreation wonderland of Lake Tahoe is packed full of information about the area's natural and human history, reservation services, bed and breakfast inns and the best restaurants. Activities from special hikes to beaches, from sled dog rides to downhill and cross country skiing are described along with detailed directions, addresses and telephone numbers. $12.95

All Roads Lead to Yosemite by Ellie Huggins
Where to Stay and Play In and Near the Park

The first of its kind guide to lodging, dining and activities in Yosemite National Park and its gateway communities of Oakhurst, Mariposa, Groveland and Lee Vining/June Lake. Learn about bed and breakfast inns, motels, lodges and restaurants plus hiking, boating, rafting, fishing, winter sports and much, much more in the park and along Highways 41, 140 and 120 East and West. Sections are color coded with maps and more than 100 photographs and illustrations. 320 pages. $13.95

Mountain Dreamers: Visionaries of Sierra Nevada Skiing
by Robert Frohlich. Photographs by Carolyn Caddes and Tom Lippert

In this handsome pictorial you will meet 28 pioneers of Sierra Nevada skiing and read their stories—like founders Dave McCoy of Mammoth Mountain and Alex Cushing and Wayne Poulsen of Squaw Valley, racers Jill Kinmont, Tamara McKinney and Jimmie Heuga and instructor Nic Fiore of Yosemite who is still teaching after 50 years at Badger Pass. With modern day portraits of the visionaries and aerials of their ski resorts, plus 80 historical photographs, this a must read for all skiers. 160 pages. Softcover: $29.95, Hardcover: $50.00

Skiing with Style: Sugar Bowl 60 Years
by Robert Frohlich and S. E. Humphries

A celebration of Sugar Bowl's 60 years. This beautiful duotone book documents how Hannes Schroll and a few families created the Sierra's first ski resort, how it was built and tells stories of decades of fun and games on the slopes. The famous Silver Belt races are remembered by a score of winners. It is illustrated with more than a hundred photos old and new, including first instructors, Bill Klein and Peter Picard, who are still skiing with style today. 112 pages. $40.

Northwest Passages from the Pen of John Muir in California, Oregon, Washington and Alaska
Designed and Illustrated by Andrea Hendrick
1988 winner of the Ben Franklin Award

Merging original woodcuts with selections of Muir's most inspirational and perceptive insights about California, Oregon, Washington and Alaska, *Northwest Passages* reveals the man who signed his name "John Muir - Earth-planet, Universe." All who seek renewal and solace in the out-of-doors will savor and cherish this book of Muir's timeless wisdom. 60 pages. $15.00

ABOUT COLDSTREAM PRESS

Ellie Huggins and Dan Wendin operate their small press from a home at the foot of Donner Pass near the Emigrant Trail. The publishing company is named for the nearby valley where thousands of emigrants hauled their wagons over the Sierra Nevada to the California gold fields. A love of the region and its rich history have led them to create books about the Sierra.

They have gathered together a team of an award winning designer and renowned photographers to realize their vision of distinctive books that introduce the special people and places of the Sierra. They seek authors to write about the history and remembrances of those who brought the excitement of winter sports to the Sierra Nevada.

Their travel guides are researched together and written by Ellie. The books describe the lodging, dining and activities of the tourist meccas of the Lake Tahoe and Yosemite regions. "One of the best parts of our research is to stay in bed and breakfast inns and to indulge in our love of special hikes and fine food."

COLDSTREAM PRESS
P.O. Box 9590
Truckee, California 96162
800.916.7450 Fax: 530.587.9081
E-Mail: dwendin@coldstreampress.com

Visit us at:
www.coldstreampress.com